YORK NOTES

# WHOSE LIFE IS IT ANYWAY?

## BRIAN CLARK

### NOTES BY ROGER MACHIN

 Longman

 York Press

The right of Roger Machin to be identified as Author of this Work
has been asserted by him in accordance with the Copyright,
Designs and Patents Act 1988

YORK PRESS
322 Old Brompton Road, London SW5 9JH

PEARSON EDUCATION LIMITED
Edinburgh Gate, Harlow,
Essex CM20 2JE, United Kingdom
Associated companies, branches and representatives throughout the world

First published 2006

10 9 8 7 6 5 4 3 2 1

ISBN–10: 1–405–83558–3
ISBN–13: 978–1–405–83558–9

Illustrated by Stephen Player
Typeset by utimestwo, Northamptonshire
Printed in China

# CONTENTS

# PREFACE

York Notes are designed to give you a broader perspective on works of literature studied at GCSE and equivalent levels. With examination requirements changing in the twenty-first century, we have made a number of significant changes to this new series. We continue to help students to reach their own interpretation of the text but York Notes now have important extra-value new features.

You will discover that York Notes are genuinely interactive. The new **Checkpoint** features will make sure that you can test your knowledge and broaden your understanding. You will also be directed to excellent websites, books and films where you can follow up ideas for yourself.

The **Resources** section has been updated and an entirely new section has been devoted to how to improve your grade. Careful reading and application of the principles laid out in the Resources section guarantee improved performance.

The **Detailed summaries** include an easy-to-follow skeleton structure of the storyline, while the section on **Language and style** has been extended to offer an in-depth discussion of the writer's techniques.

The Contents page shows the structure of this study guide. However, there is no need to read from the beginning to the end as you would with a novel, play or poem. Use the Notes in the way that suits you. Our aim is to help you with your understanding of the work, not to dictate how you should learn.

Our authors are practising English teachers and examiners who have used their experience to offer a whole range of **Examiner's secrets** – useful hints to encourage exam success.

The author of these Notes is Roger Machin M.Phil., English teacher, examiner and author of many study texts and guides to literature.

The text used in these Notes is the Heinemann Plays edition, 1993, with an introduction and notes by Ray Speakman.

## PART ONE

## INTRODUCTION

# HOW TO STUDY A PLAY

Plays are written to be performed, so as well as reading the text, try to see a production, on television, video, DVD or, best of all, on stage. A performance will give you a real sense of what the playwright intended and will bring the play alive for you.

When you study a text, there are certain aspects to look out for:

❶ THE PLOT: a play is a carefully constructed story. Each event that happens has a bearing on the whole play.

❷ THE CHARACTERS: these are the individuals taking part in the 'story' of the play. You will gain an impression of them as the play unfolds. You may find that you like or dislike some, think some are foolish and others noble. The characters may change, or your perception of them may alter, during the play.

❸ THE THEMES: these are the ideas in the play, the issues the playwright wishes you to consider, or the points he or she would like to make, e.g. 'life is fragile' or 'ambition can have tragic consequences'.

❹ THE SETTING: this is the time and place that the playwright chooses for the play.

❺ THE LANGUAGE: the writer's choice of words and phrases which are deliberately chosen to help convey characters and ideas.

❻ STAGING AND PERFORMANCE: the type of stage, lighting, scenery, sound effects, acting style and delivery are all considered carefully by the director when a play is produced.

A director has the difficult job of looking at how a playwright has presented the play, and then interpreting it for the stage.

These York Notes will help you to understand what the play is about and will guide you in forming your own interpretation. Do not expect the study of the play to be easy: plays are not written for examination purposes but to be performed!

**CHECK THE NET**

A production of *Whose Life is it Anyway?* was performed at the Comedy Theatre in London in 2005. You can find a reference to it on the theatre's website: **www. theambassadors. com/comedy/info**

**CHECK THE FILM**

You could have a look at either the 1972 Granada TV play or the 1981 Hollywood film. Seeing a staged version will greatly help your understanding.

| AUTHOR – LIFE AND WORKS | CONTEXT |
|---|---|
| | **1928** Alexander Fleming realises that bacteria are killed by penicillin. Leads to development of antibiotics which save millions of lives |
| **1932** Brian Clark born in Bournemouth | |
| | **1939–45** Second World War. Antibiotics used extensively for the first time |
| | **1945–51** Clement Attlee is Labour prime minister. Sets up the Welfare State, which guarantees access to basic standards of living for all. The National Health Service is a crucial part of this |
| | **1950** Smoking is identified for the first time as a direct cause of lung cancer |
| | **1960s** Development of intensive care units that maintain life through artificial ventilation |
| | **1964–70** Harold Wilson is Labour prime minister. Predicts a future forged by the 'white heat of technology' |
| **1966–70** Staff tutor in drama at the University of Hull | |
| | **1967** Hospice movement is founded in response to growing numbers of patients living with terminal conditions. First human heart transplant carried out by Dr Christiaan Barnard |
| | **1970–74** Edward Heath is Conservative prime minister. Takes Britain into the European Community |
| **1972** *Whose Life is it Anyway?* screened by Granada TV | |
| **1974** *A Follower for Emily* | |

## AUTHOR – LIFE AND WORKS

**1978** *Whose Life is it Anyway?* premiers as a stage play at the Mermaid Theatre, London. Tom Conti plays Ken. Clark adapts James Herriot's *All Creatures Great and Small* for television; the series is an enormous popular success

**1979** *Can You Hear Me at the Back?* produced in London

**1981** *Whose Life is it Anyway?* is filmed in Hollywood; Richard Dreyfuss stars as Ken. *Whose Life is it Anyway?* appears on Broadway with a female lead. The character of Ken Harrison is replaced by Claire Harrison

**1986** *The Petition* opens in New York

**1990** *Hopping to Byzantium* is produced in Germany

**2001** *In Pursuit of Eve* premiers in London

**2005** *Whose Life is it Anyway?* is produced at the Comedy Theatre, London; Kim Cattrall from *Sex and the City* plays Claire Harrison; Peter Hall directs it

## CONTEXT

**1978** Louise Brown is the first 'test-tube baby'

**1979–90** Margaret Thatcher is Conservative prime minister. Period of conflict in British society. The Welfare State is challenged and partially dismantled

**1980** World Health Organization formally announces eradication of deadly smallpox virus

**1985** Development of keyhole surgery

**1996** Dolly the sheep cloned

**2000** Euthanasia legalised in Holland

**2003** Mapping of the human genome completed

**DID YOU KNOW?**

It is not unheard of for playwrights to rewrite their plays. It is, however, very unusual for them to change the sex of their leading character, as Clark did with *Whose Life is it Anyway?*

**CHECK THE BOOK**

If you want to compare the original *Whose Life is it Anyway?* with the version performed in 2005, starring Kim Cattrall as Claire Harrison, you can find the 2005 text published by Amber Lane Press, the company Clark himself set up in 1978 to promote new playwrights and their work.

# SETTING AND BACKGROUND

## BRIAN CLARK AND SOCIAL JUSTICE

When Brian Clark was born in the south of England in the early 1930s, living conditions for most British people were very poor. At the end of the Second World War, however, popular movements that had for decades demanded better conditions for ordinary people finally had their moment. A Labour government was elected in a landslide victory with the mandate to end misery and hardship and to provide a basic standard of living for all. It was a time of great hope and monumental promises. The broadest of these was to deliver social justice. Citizens had rights. When they were young they had a right to be educated; when they were sick they should be given access to health care; when they were thrown out of work they should be given a living wage; when they were old they should be secure. These sorts of promises and the way they might be fulfilled have been the subject for political debate ever since.

Brian Clark is a dramatic commentator on these social issues. His plays are intensely personal but there is always the sense of the wider context. In *Whose Life is it Anyway?* Clark's focus is on personal suffering, imprisonment, thwarted sexuality, the struggle for self-determination. But behind all this is the issue of social justice. What should society do to help the individual? How should society respond? How should it exercise its responsibility to bring about a just and proper conclusion for each person? Judge Millhouse answers this question in the case of Ken Harrison at the end of the play. Society, for Brian Clark, is there to help and this is its function. He is a man of his time, optimistic about the role of the state in the life of the individual.

## PUBLIC HEALTH

Over the course of the twentieth century, the state of medical knowledge progressed with great speed. Conditions and diseases that humankind had feared for thousands of years were either controlled or completely eradicated by developments in drugs, surgical procedures and care techniques. Hand in hand with this new medical understanding came state-regulated health services that guaranteed access to care. No longer was health the preserve only of those who could afford to pay. After the Second World War, other developments also helped improve the quality of the lives of ordinary people. Housing, sanitation, provision for old age, food hygiene, regulation of working hours: all these factors and more meant that the harsh and cruel conditions of an unregulated, unprotected life touched fewer and fewer people.

## MEDICAL PROGRESS AND ETHICS

Developments in medical care and social welfare raised questions by the 1960s that would previously have been unthinkable. Foremost amongst these was the problem of what to do in the case of people being kept artificially alive. Intensive care units were in widespread use by the time Brian Clark wrote *Whose Life is it Anyway?* For the first time in human history, life could be preserved even in the absence of the function of the brain and the vital organs. The problem in these cases often became not how to save life but how and sometimes whether it should be maintained.

## THE RIGHT TO DIE DEBATE

The issues that arose in the sixties are now relevant to many more people as medical science prolongs life where before it would have ended. The public discussion of these issues has become known as the 'right to die' debate. The debate centres around the rights of individuals to make choices about when they die. It is complicated by the fact that many of those who might wish to die are no longer in a fit state either to end their own lives or to communicate their wishes. And there are still important groups, notably the Catholic Church, who oppose the individual's right to determine their time of death at all.

When a person's brain ceases to function it is, of course, impossible for them to express an opinion about the time of death. Permission to withdraw life support is usually requested from the nearest relatives. The husband or wife of the patient has priority over the rest of the family. The trouble is that it is not always clear whether

**CHECK THE NET**

Look at the official NHS website, **www.nhs.uk**. You can find descriptions here of the NHS in 1978 when the play was first performed. Click on 'A history of the NHS' on the main homepage.

**DID YOU KNOW?**

Terri Schiavo spent more than a decade in a persistent vegetative state. In 1998 her husband began a long struggle to persuade the courts to remove the feeding tube keeping her alive. He was bitterly opposed by Terri's parents, but eventually her tube was removed in March 2005, and she died a fortnight later.

**CHECK THE NET**

You can learn more about Christopher Reeve's life and accident, together with the work done by the Christopher Reeve Foundation, at **www. christopherreeve. org**

or not irreversible brain death has occurred. Where there is disagreement over this, a long and painful legal battle can take place. This happened in the United States in the case of Terri Schiavo (1998–2005).

Those suffering brain death have a functioning body but their mind has ceased to be active. Patients with major or total paralysis (quadriplegics and paraplegics) have fully active minds but their bodies no longer function normally. Notwithstanding this, many sufferers are able to live rich and fulfilling lives. Christopher Reeve, the American actor who played Superman in the Hollywood films, is the most conspicuous recent example. He was paralysed in a riding accident yet campaigned actively until his death in 2004 on such issues as stem cell research that offered hope for people in his condition. Stephen Hawking, the Nobel Prize winning physicist, is another case of someone whose severe disability has not prevented a brilliant life. Ken Harrison, the hero of *Whose Life is it Anyway?*, is a quadriplegic but does not share the attitude demonstrated by the likes of Reeve and Hawking. He wants to die and will do so if treatment is withdrawn. Most doctors, unlike Dr Emerson in the play, will now accept the wishes of a patient like Ken. The most recent example of doctors not doing so came in a case heard by the High Court in 2002. Miss B, as she had to be called, asked to have her life-support system switched off. Her doctors refused to do so because they believed she was not of sound mind and her condition could be improved with the right treatment. The High Court ordered Miss B's doctors to respect her wishes and she was allowed to die.

The doctors refused to act on Miss B's instructions because they argued she was insane. She proved, however, that this was not the case, and the doctors were obliged to follow her instructions to withdraw her treatment and allow her to die. Ken has to do the same in the play and he achieves the same result. It remains the case, nevertheless, that the depressed, insane or senile may not under the law order their doctors to allow them to die. This is, of course, a necessary safeguard to prevent people from ending their own lives when, if they were thinking rationally, they would not actually wish to.

Miss B's case aside, there are not many cases left like Ken's any more. If an obviously sane patient requests that life support be removed, then doctors have instructions from their ruling body, the British Medical Association (BMA), to follow those orders. The debate about the right to die has now moved on to those cases where patients are not able to die easily without some form of assistance. Most patients in this sort of condition have lost bodily control and cannot therefore commit suicide. This means that they may request a partner or a doctor to administer some life-ending dose of medication. They may do this at the time they wish to die or they may have left a 'living will' giving instructions on what to do should they lose the power to communicate. The best-known British case of this was that of Diane Pretty, who suffered from incurable motor neurone disease. As her illness became worse, Diane Pretty saw nothing ahead of her but an unbearable life concluded by a slow, painful and undignified death. Unable to end her own life, she requested that either her husband or her doctors be given immunity from prosecution if they agreed to help her die. The British courts refused her that permission, and she was also denied by the highest court available to her, the European Court of Human Rights. Eventually, Diane Pretty died in the way she had feared.

In the UK, anyone who assists a terminally ill person to commit suicide risks prosecution for murder. An alternative option for those in Mrs Pretty's situation is to go abroad to Holland, Belgium or Switzerland, where assisted suicide is not illegal.

Improvements in public health and in medical knowledge suggest that debates over the right to die are set to continue. Opponents of assisted suicide argue that it is a slippery slope that may end up with unscrupulous people pressurising unwanted relatives into suicide. They also argue that medicine is now able to prevent much of the pain suffered by the ill, and that where there is life there is hope. Those in support point to cases like those of Diane Pretty and argue that it is inhumane to condemn them to an appalling life and an agonising death. The arguments remain similar to those dramatised by Brian Clark in his play over thirty years ago.

 **DID YOU KNOW?**

In January 2006 Anne Turner, a retired English doctor suffering from a degenerative disease, took her life with the help of doctors at a clinic in Switzerland.

**Now take a break!**

**1**

Ken Harrison lies paralysed in a hospital bed. Sister Anderson, Nurse Sadler and John, the orderly, attend to him on their morning rounds. Ken's conversation is cynical yet humorous.

**2**

Dr Scott and Dr Emerson check up on Ken. Although his physical condition is stable, the doctors are concerned by his 'agitated' state of mind. Dr Scott intends to administer Valium but Ken refuses to take it.

**3**

John flirts energetically with Nurse Sadler in the sluice room. The fertile vitality of this scene contrasts with the living death being endured by Ken across the hospital corridor.

**4**

Dr Scott tells Dr Emerson that Ken has refused the Valium. Dr Emerson is impatient with this and injects the drug himself, against Ken's wishes.

**5**

Mrs Boyle, the medical social worker, attempts to help Ken find a way out of his 'depression'. Ken is infuriated by her refusal to listen to him properly.

**6**

Ken explains to Dr Scott his reasons for no longer wishing to live. She tries to resist his arguments but is slowly becoming convinced by them.

**7**

Philip Hill starts to examine the legal issues surrounding Ken's potential release from hospital. Dr Emerson tells Hill that Ken is not mentally sound and must therefore remain in care. The relationship between John and Nurse Sadler continues to develop.

**8**

Dr Travers, the hospital psychiatrist, advises Dr Emerson on how to use the Mental Health Act in order to keep Ken at the hospital. Dr Emerson explains his plans to Dr Scott. Dr Travers makes his assessment of Ken.

**9**

Dr Scott and Philip Hill return from a date during which they have discussed Ken's case. Dr Scott visits Ken and is both friendly and supportive.

**10**

Peter Kershaw, Ken's barrister, and Mr Hill tell Ken that an appeal against his detention might take a year. They decide instead to apply for an immediate writ of habeas corpus on the basis that Ken is being held against his will without good reason.

**11**

John and Nurse Sadler prepare Ken's room for the legal hearing. In conversation with both Ken and Philip Hill, Dr Emerson shows that his position remains unchanged.

**12**

Judge Millhouse hears statements from Dr Emerson and Dr Barr, a psychiatrist from another hospital who considers Ken sane. The judge then questions Ken himself and discovers him to be sound of mind. He grants the writ of habeas corpus, thereby clearing the way for Ken to die.

**Consultant physician**
Dr Emerson
*Wants to detain Ken in hospital*

**Judge**
Justice Millhouse
*Orders Ken's release from hospital*

**Hospital's barrister**
Andrew Eden
*Argues against Ken's release*

**Ken's barrister**
Peter Kershaw
*Argues for Ken's release*

**Consultant psychiatrist**
Dr Travers
*Diagnoses Ken as mentally unsound*

**Consultant psychiatrist**
Dr Barr
*Diagnoses Ken as sane*

**Medical social worker**
Mrs Boyle
*Tries to convince Ken to adapt and live*

**Junior registrar**
Dr Scott
*Encourages Ken to decide his own fate*

**Ward sister**
Sister Anderson
*Wants Ken to live*

**Ken's solicitor**
Philip Hill
*Supports Ken's right to die*

*Ken's carers*           **Ward orderly** John

**Trainee Nurse**
Nurse Sadler

## PART TWO

## SUMMARIES

## GENERAL SUMMARY

### ACT I

The first morning of the play. Ken Harrison lies paralysed in a hospital bed, attended to by Sister Anderson and the inexperienced Nurse Sadler. Ken likes Nurse Sadler; he also likes John, the orderly who comes in to shave him. Dr Scott, a junior registrar, checks up on Ken's condition. Ken indicates to her that he feels his life is not worth living, a position Dr Scott does not yet acknowledge.

Dr Emerson, a consultant physician, examines Ken. Ken refuses to engage with Emerson's insistently positive tone and is disparaging about the value of his own life. Emerson is disturbed by Ken's attitude and suggests an increase in the drug prescription and a visit by the medical social worker, Mrs Boyle. After Dr Emerson's departure, Dr Scott tries to give Ken a small dose of Valium but he persuades her not to.

The action moves to the sluice room. John is vigorously advancing his sexual case to Nurse Sadler. She resists yet seems amused and attracted. In the meantime, Dr Scott tells Dr Emerson that Ken has refused his Valium. Emerson has no patience with Ken's reasoning and seems more concerned that Dr Scott has not asserted her authority. He injects Ken with a high dose of the drug himself, to Ken's fury.

The second morning of the play opens in the same way as the first, with Sister Anderson and Nurse Sadler attending to Ken. Ken asks Sister to contact his solicitor. She mistakenly believes this is a sign that Ken is planning for the future; in fact he intends to ask his solicitor to help him leave the hospital so he can die. Mrs Boyle, the medical social worker, arrives to convince Ken that life will still be worth living despite his paralysis. Ken is enraged by the way she treats him and becomes so furious that oxygen needs to be administered.

 **DID YOU KNOW?**

*Whose Life is it Anyway?* was turned into a Hollywood film in 1981. It was not a commercial success and is now rarely seen.

Dr Scott is now taking a markedly personal interest in Ken's case. Ken is attracted to her, and a heightened consciousness of his sexual impotence leads him more generally to consider the fact that he cannot direct any serious aspect of his existence. These feelings he expresses with force and clarity to Dr Scott, whose attempts to contradict him are by now becoming feeble. Unlike Emerson and Mrs Boyle, Dr Scott has an open mind and Ken's calmly delivered, rational arguments are winning her over.

**DID YOU KNOW?**

Ken's condition, quadriplegia, is a paralysis of all four limbs, i.e. a complete loss of feeling and movement in his arms and legs.

## ACT II

Another new day arrives, and this time the action begins in the afternoon. Philip Hill, Ken's solicitor, has come to see him in order, he thinks, to finalise Ken's claim for compensation. Instead Ken tells Hill he wants the hospital to release him to die. Hill agrees to discuss the issue with Dr Emerson. John continues his energetic seduction of Nurse Sadler in the sluice room. Philip Hill has a brief meeting with Dr Emerson. Emerson dismisses Ken's case but is forced to concede that the only way he can legally retain Ken is by judging him insane. Hill says he will employ his own psychiatrist to make a judgement.

Dr Emerson contacts the hospital psychiatrist, Dr Travers, who advises him on the provisions of the Mental Health Act. To keep Ken in hospital, an external psychiatrist will have to add his signature to Dr Emerson's. Emerson informs Dr Scott that he intends to detain Ken against his will on the basis of mental instability. Dr Scott is entirely opposed to Dr Emerson's reasoning, his ethics and his plans. Dr Travers assesses Ken's mental condition. Ken emerges as rational, sane and intelligent; nevertheless, Travers is unconvinced.

The action moves forward to the evening of the third day. Mr Hill and Dr Scott return from dinner resolved to assist Ken in his attempt to die. Ken tells Dr Scott that he is starting to feel human again but cannot go on living in his current condition.

Another new day and Ken is visited by Hill and Peter Kershaw, his barrister. They explain to a horrified Ken that an appeal against his detention may take up to a year. They then suggest that he appeals for a writ of habeas corpus. If a judge were prepared to issue the writ, the hospital would be forced to release him and he would be free to die. Hill and Kershaw promise to find a judge to hear the case.

The final day of the play. As Nurse Sadler and John put out the chairs for the hearing in Ken's room, Ken picks up on their intimacy and teases them. Sister, Dr Scott and Dr Emerson exchange a few words with Ken before the hearing begins. Outside Ken's room, Emerson and Hill discuss the case and its implications for the authority of doctors. Judge Millhouse then arrives and the case is heard.

**CHECK THE BOOK**

*In Last Rights: The Struggle Over the Right to Die*, Sue Woodman provides a broad and balanced review of the right to die debate. It is filled with personal details that illustrate all sides of the argument.

Dr Emerson is the first to present his evidence. He asserts that Ken is clinically depressed because of his trauma and is therefore unable to make sound judgements. Dr Barr, a psychiatrist appointed by Ken's legal team, then gives evidence that contradicts Emerson. Consequently, Judge Millhouse is forced to question Ken himself. Ken speaks to the judge as convincingly as he did to Dr Travers. Judge Millhouse comes to the conclusion that Ken is sane and must not be prevented from following the dictates of his reason. He issues the writ of habeas corpus and Ken is free to die. Dr Emerson tells Ken that he can remain in his hospital bed to do so.

**Now take a break!**

## DETAILED SUMMARIES

### PART ONE [pp. 1–4] – Ken, Sister Anderson, Nurse Sadler and John

**❶ Four characters are introduced.**

**❷ Ken's physical condition is revealed.**

Ken Harrison lies paralysed but awake in a hospital bed. It is morning, and two nurses enter his room. The older and senior nurse, Sister Anderson, introduces Nurse Sadler, a student. Ken apologises to Nurse Sadler for being unable to shake her hand and says she will have to make do with his 'backside' (p. 1). As part of his treatment, the nurses roll Ken over and massage him. Ken tells the women he used to dream about getting this sort of personal attention.

Sister is called outside by a phone call and Ken is left alone with Nurse Sadler. She tells him her first name is Kay. He replies that she had better refer to herself as 'Nurse Sadler' when talking to her patients. We learn that she is in her final week of training school and is looking forward to leaving. She asks Ken if he used to be a teacher. Ken tells her not to talk in the past tense, as she is now 'part of the optimism industry' (p. 2). We discover that Ken has suffered a 'ruptured spinal column'.

> **CHECKPOINT 1**
>
> What are the differences between the ways Sister and Nurse Sadler respond to Ken?

Sister returns and the two women roll Ken back over and remake his bed. Ken tells Sister he has taken an immediate liking to Nurse Sadler. Sister tells Ken she heard he slept well the previous night. Ken responds jokingly that he went out skateboarding – and that he was the skateboard.

The two nurses leave Ken alone and discuss his condition. We discover that Ken has been in his room for four months and will soon be transferred to a long-stay hospital. He will never recover from his injuries. John, an orderly, passes the nurses on his way to give Ken a shave.

## Ken's humour

The opening of the play gives us an early glimpse of Ken's sense of humour. We have seen how he introduces his 'backside' (p. 1) to Nurse Sadler and jokes about being a 'skateboard' (p. 3) during the night for an imaginary friend. Much of his conversation has a sexual edge to it and his obvious physical incapacity makes his repeated sexual innuendo (double meanings about sex) both darkly humorous and pathetic. While the nurses lower his bed he pretends to be descending in a lift through 'Obstetrics, Gynaecology, Lingerie, Rubber wear' (p. 1). He makes frequent jokes based on his own sexual impotence. Sister tells Nurse Sadler to balance Ken carefully on the bed or she will 'have him on the floor'. Ken replies, 'Have me on the floor Sister please. Have me on the floor' (p. 1). When Sister returns from her phone call, she asks Nurse Sadler whether she has finished. Ken pretends she is talking to him and says, 'I haven't started her yet!' (p. 3).

Ken's humour is self-deprecating. He is prepared to use himself as the butt of the jokes he makes. He is not afraid to laugh at himself and the position he finds himself in. He jokes about sex because he finds it ludicrous to imagine himself in any sexual situation.

### CHECKPOINT 2

What other examples of Ken's self-deprecating humour can you find in this section?

### GLOSSARY

**part of the optimism industry** Ken believes his carers act in a way that is falsely hopeful

**ruptured spinal column** Ken has broken his back and is paralysed from the neck down

**Obstetrics, Gynaecology** medical terms to describe the study of childbirth and the female reproductive system

**Lingerie, Rubber wear** women's underwear and fetish wear. The joke is on Ken since he knows there is no future for him in these areas

## PART TWO [pp. 4–10] – Ken talks to John, Dr Scott and Nurse Sadler

❶ Ken expresses negative feelings both about himself and senior hospital staff.

❷ John shows humanity in his dealings with Ken.

❸ Dr Scott talks playfully with Ken but becomes concerned for him.

❹ Ken shows distaste for 'professionalism'.

John arrives to give Ken a shave. Ken jokingly talks to John as if he is a gardener tidying up a lawn and asks if he can provide some fertiliser to help him grow. John picks up the **metaphor** and says he is only a labourer and cannot take important decisions. Ken says John must at least be in charge of the compost heap, which is where he thinks he should be.

Sister puts her head round the door to tell John not to be too long as there is to be a consultant's round later in the morning. Ken responds to this news **ironically**. He says there is to be a 'visitation of the Gods' (p. 5). He feels that the consultants have a too high opinion of themselves. When he learns that one of them has left to get married, he says it must be to a lorry driver.

> **CHECKPOINT 3**
>
> Why do you think Ken is so fond of John?

> **CHECKPOINT 4**
>
> What does Ken's use of metaphors suggest about his personality?

John picks him up for his sarcasm. Ken denies this and says he is jealous: 'From where I'm lying, if you can make it at all – even with your right hand – it would be heaven' (p. 5).

Ken changes the subject to talk about John. John tells him he is trying to go professional with a steel band. Ken thinks that making music out of scrap is a great idea and asks John to knock a tune out of him. John taps Ken lightly up and down his body and sings a tune.

Dr Scott, a junior registrar, arrives in Ken's room. She is the most senior medical figure we have met so far. She immediately demonstrates a certain tolerance by asking John not to stop his musical performance on Ken's body. John, however, leaves soon afterwards and Dr Scott comments that Ken is 'bright and chirpy this morning' (p. 6). Ken makes an ironic response and Dr Scott replies in a similar tone. She seems unwilling to maintain the breeziness of her greeting. She puts a stethoscope to Ken's chest but his singing and talking prevents her from hearing anything. He tells her that the first and second heart sounds are the result of his heart being broken in two. Each side of his heart, though, is 'bravely yearning for a woman in a white coat' (p. 7).

Ken then returns to the idea of the consultants being like gods. He imagines Dr Emerson about to 'sweep in here like Zeus from Olympus, with his attendant nymphs and swains' (p. 7). Dr Scott defends Dr Emerson and says he worked hard to save Ken's life when he first arrived. Ken apologises, but wonders whether all the effort was worthwhile.

Dr Scott is now concerned at Ken's state of mind. She leaves him alone and tells Sister she is going to prescribe Valium to calm his nerves.

---

### Gardeners and gods

Ken likes to use metaphors. He thinks of John as a gardener and himself as vegetable waste for the compost heap. He portrays Dr Emerson as Zeus, king of the gods, and the nursing staff as 'nymphs and swains' (p. 7). One of these is Nurse Sadler, whom he sees as an 'acolyte' (p. 8) and later a 'vestal virgin' (p. 9).

---

**GLOSSARY**

**even with your right hand** Ken says jokily that he is jealous of any man who can have sex with a woman since he cannot even masturbate

**nymphs and swains** beautiful young women and young male lovers, depicted here as devoted followers of the gods

**acolyte** a follower; an assistant in a religious service

**vestal virgin** a virgin dedicated to the goddess Vesta in ancient Rome and vowed to chastity

Nurse Sadler goes into Ken's room with a feeding cup. With mock drama he calls her an 'acolyte' (p. 8). She does not understand him and gives him some milky coffee which he does not like. Ken tells Nurse Sadler that she has a 'lovely body' (p. 9) and she is temporarily embarrassed. He apologises to her sincerely yet makes things comically worse by calling her a 'vestal virgin' (p. 9).

Ken asks her what made her become a nurse. She gives a short reply and asks Ken what made him become a sculptor. This annoys Ken since he feels she is deflecting him in a 'professional' way. 'Patients are requested not to ask for credit for their intelligence,' Ken says, 'as refusal often offends' (p. 10). Sister then opens the door and tells Nurse Sadler to finish what she is doing since Dr Emerson has arrived.

> **CHECKPOINT 5**
>
> Locate the word 'professional' on p. 6 and then on p. 10. How does the first use differ from the second?

---

### Talking to Ken

Ken often feels patronised by the way people speak to him. When Sister introduces Nurse Sadler she does so by saying, 'A new face for you today' (p. 1). Dr Scott's first words to him are: 'You're bright and chirpy this morning' (p. 6). Neither woman would speak like this to an equal. When Ken asks Nurse Sadler a question about her work, she refuses to answer it properly. It is as if Ken is a young child and his carers have become parents or teachers. He is refused access to the adult world.

---

## PART THREE [pp. 10–15] – Dr Emerson, Dr Scott and Ken

1. Dr Emerson makes a medical diagnosis of Ken.

2. Ken forces Dr Emerson to be honest with him about his future.

3. Ken persuades Dr Scott not to give him the Valium.

Ken answers Dr Emerson's greeting with an **ironic** reply. Dr Emerson ignores it and makes a quick medical diagnosis which turns out to be positive. He tells Ken that he should soon be in a stable medical condition. Ken uses this as his cue to ask whether he will soon be discharged. Dr Emerson says he will be transferred to a 'more comfortable unit'. Ken remarks drily that 'you only grow the vegetables here – the vegetable store is somewhere else' (p. 11). His **metaphor** reminds us of his earlier comment to John about being thrown on the compost heap. Dr Emerson, in the professional way that Ken dislikes, tries to ignore what has been said but Ken is prepared to force the issue. He compels Dr Emerson to admit that he will never regain the use of his limbs. Having done so, he thanks Dr Emerson for his honesty, as if the truth is something in short supply. Dr Emerson tells Ken not to brood on his troubles and leaves.

**CHECK THE NET**

You can read an interview with Brian Clark about the recent staging of the play by going to **www. independent.co. uk**. Use the advanced search engine and type in the title of the play and the date of the article (6 January 2005).

### Irony

Much of Ken's speech is ironic. He tells Dr Scott that he is making himself 'beautiful' for her (p. 6). Later he calls her a 'highly qualified nurse' (p. 13) and tells Dr Emerson that he has been 'racing around all over the place' (p. 10). Ken doesn't believe he could ever be beautiful; he is teasing when he calls Dr Scott a nurse; and he is aware that Dr Emerson realises he cannot run. He dramatically lampoons reality to show his listeners that he understands it and can deal with it. He uses irony as a way of asserting his will without becoming aggressive. He stops using irony when he becomes serious or when he gets angry.

**GLOSSARY**

**Patients are requested ... as refusal often offends** signs in shops used to advise customers not to ask for credit as it would not be given. Ken feels his intelligence is dismissed in just the same way

Dr Emerson and Dr Scott talk in the corridor about Ken. Dr Emerson says that there is a high demand for the kind of care Ken is receiving and that they should aim to have him moved in no more than a month. He tells Dr Scott that she might have to increase Ken's Valium dose and then rushes off to a meeting. He is trying to get funding for a new heart monitoring unit.

**CHECKPOINT 6**

How does Dr Emerson see his responsibilities?

Dr Scott takes the Valium prescription in to give to Ken. Ken tells her that he enjoyed the conversation with Dr Emerson because it made him feel human again. In other words, he appreciated being spoken to honestly. Now, he says, Dr Scott is going to spoil things by tranquillising herself. This is another one of those provocative verbal tricks by which Ken forces people to take notice of him. He tells Dr Scott that she feels powerless to help him and is made unhappy by this fact. Therefore, he argues, she is about to give him a pill that will keep him quiet so that she can relax.

Dr Scott says that Ken is not telling 'the whole story' (p. 14). She feels that he may need the Valium to help him calm down. Only then, she feels, will he be able to take a measured and rational view of his situation. Ken disagrees. He says that all he has is his consciousness. It is surely up to him to use it as he wishes. He manages to persuade her to take the tablet away.

## PART FOUR [pp. 15–18] – Nurse Sadler and John in the sluice room

❶ John flirts comically with Nurse Sadler.

❷ They express conflicting attitudes about the work done by the hospital.

Nurse Sadler is working by herself in the sluice room when John creeps in and grabs her by the waist. When she tells him not to, he says he could not help himself – she is so irresistible. Nurse Sadler behaves as if she would rather be getting on with her job than flirting with John. In fact, she asks him why he's working in a critical unit at all if he can't take it seriously. He replies that what the hospital staff do is not so important since the critical unit is just the 'ante-room of the morgue' (p. 16). He also makes the point that the money being spent on Ken would be better spent saving children's lives in poorer countries.

But John is actually far more interested in Nurse Sadler than in these broader issues and he soon steers the conversation back to her. He compliments her and then tries to get a date. When she tells him she is too busy studying he tells her he can give her a good 'anatomy lesson' (p. 17). The anatomy he cares about, of course, is limited to Nurse Sadler's body and he expresses this in a jokey song. The energy and physicality surrounding these two provides a dramatic contrast with Ken's paralysis. The scene is interrupted by Sister, whom Nurse Sadler bumps into as she is trying to escape. She deals briskly with both of them and a clinical, professional atmosphere is re-established.

> **CHECKPOINT 7**
>
> Does the contrast between Ken and John made plain by this scene prove that Ken has nothing to live for?

### A real man?

John and Ken both find Nurse Sadler attractive and neither has any hesitation in letting her know. Ken's flirtation is **ironic**, however, because he believes there is no way it can lead anywhere. John's advances are humorous (he wants to keep things light) but they are nevertheless in complete earnest. He knows there is real potential for him to be successful. So whilst Ken is forced to imitate life, John can get on and really live it.

> **GLOSSARY**
>
> **ante-room of the morgue** waiting room of the mortuary. John believes the unit is simply preparing patients for death

## PART FIVE [pp. 18–23] – Disagreement over the Valium prescription

**1** Dr Emerson considers financial matters.

**2** Dr Scott explains why she did not give the Valium to Ken.

**3** Dr Emerson says the drug should have been given.

**4** He administers the drug in spite of Ken's protests.

**5** Dr Scott and Sister consider the issue of detachment.

Dr Emerson is on the phone to a colleague named Jenkins and is trying to convince him that a costly new piece of equipment will save the hospital money in the long run. This is some small indication of the pressure felt by medical administrators as they try to cope with issues not necessarily related to immediate patient care. It may make a reader or viewer of the play a little more sympathetic to Dr Emerson in the debate that is to follow.

This debate is caused by Ken's unwillingness to take the Valium Dr Scott has prescribed. Dr Scott is sympathetic with Ken's position because she believes it to be a rational response to his circumstances. All he has is his mind and he wants to keep it clear. Dr Emerson, however, appears at this stage to have little time for his patients' opinions. He is concerned only to establish that the initial decision made by his colleague and himself was considered and professional. He tells Dr Scott that when she prescribed the drug she thought Ken needed it. He reminds her that she made a 'careful and responsible decision' with which he, as the senior doctor, agreed. He is therefore surprised that 'in spite of two qualified opinions', Dr Scott, he says, has accepted 'the decision of someone completely unqualified to take it' (p. 19).

| CHECKPOINT 8 |
| --- |
| What reasons can you think of for Dr Emerson's rather dismissive behaviour at this precise point in the play? |

### Playing God

Dr Emerson dismisses Ken's objections because he feels that Ken is not medically qualified to express them. He appears at this stage to feel that his authority alone should be sufficient to guarantee the obedience of his patients.

Dr Scott refuses to accept that Dr Emerson's professional seniority is enough to prove him right automatically. She agrees that Ken is unqualified but points out that 'he is the one affected' (p. 19). Since she is therefore refusing to bow to his simple assertion of authority, Dr Emerson is forced to counter with a more sophisticated argument. He tells his colleague that qualified hospital staff are 'objective' (p. 19) and know more 'about drugs and their effects' (p. 20). He points out that Ken didn't protest when he was administered 'aminophylline or the huge stat dose of cortisone' (p. 20) on his admission as an emergency patient. He argues that the Valium will help Ken to relax and turn his mind to coping with the real problems lying ahead. Without the drug, Dr Emerson feels, Ken will remain in a depressed, irrational state, one in which he is unable to use his 'full consciousness' (p. 20).

Dr Emerson's position therefore becomes more credible. We feel able to agree with him that sometimes depressed people can overcome their condition with the right medication and then go on to live productively and happily without drugs.

Dr Emerson feels he has successfully made his point and he phones Sister Anderson to tell her to prepare a Valium syringe. He tells Dr Scott that Ken is an 'intelligent, sensitive and articulate man' (p. 21) but that this should not affect her professional judgement. Dr Scott's body language suggests she is unconvinced by this and they part with the issue unresolved, at least so far as she is concerned.

Dr Emerson now takes the Valium syringe from Sister and goes into Ken's room with the intention of administering the drug. Ken tells him that he does not want the Valium because he has 'decided not to stay alive' (p. 22). Dr Emerson is unable to accept this and informs Ken that his depression makes him unqualified to make decisions over his own life and death; instead Ken must learn to rely on the judgement of his doctors. Ken suggests that his depression is a perfectly natural response to his situation. Dr Emerson agrees with this and tells him that this is precisely why he needs the Valium. He injects the drug against Ken's will and leaves. Ken is furious at this but soon loses consciousness.

---

**CHECKPOINT 9**

What do we learn about Dr Scott's character?

---

**GLOSSARY**

**aminophylline … cortisone** medication given to patients in the emergency ward. Obviously Ken could not have objected to these drugs since he was unconscious when they were administered

**EXAMINER'S SECRET**

Show the examiner you understand this complex ethical debate by presenting both sides in a reasonable way. Neither side is so weak that it deserves dismissal.

## Depression

The disagreement between Ken and Dr Emerson centres at this stage on their different responses to depression. Ken feels his depression is an entirely rational and permanent response to the appalling circumstances in which he now finds himself. Dr Emerson sees that same depression as the natural but temporary reaction of a massively disconcerted mind. Ken, therefore, refuses the Valium because he prefers rational depression to contented fantasy. Dr Emerson forces the drug on him in the hope it will cure his depression and enable him 'to find a new way of living' (p. 22).

The action now crosses to a discussion already under way between Sister Anderson and Dr Scott. Dr Scott appears to have been explaining the conflict she feels between her sense of duty and her desire to uphold Ken's rights. She playfully dismisses Sister's advice not to get personally involved. It is impossible, she suggests, to be completely detached, to treat patients in an entirely 'professional' manner. She points out that even Dr Emerson is 'as involved with Mr Harrison as if he were his father' (p. 23). The conversation is interrupted by the arrival of Nurse Sadler, who appears flushed.

**CHECKPOINT 10**

Is it a good thing that Dr Emerson is like a father to Ken?

> ## Involvement
>
> The key word in this little section is 'involved' (p. 23). Sister and Dr Emerson get involved with Ken just so far as is needed to improve his medical condition. Dr Scott becomes involved with his personal and emotional needs. The approach adopted by Sister and Dr Emerson is probably necessary if the hospital is not to grind to a halt. Dr Scott's level of involvement, however, is what Ken wants and needs.

## PART SIX [pp. 24–32] – Ken meets the medical social worker

**1** **Ken asks Sister to call his solicitor.**

**2** **Mrs Boyle tries to convince Ken that life is still worth living.**

**3** **Ken is distressed by Mrs Boyle's professionalism.**

**4** **Sister and Nurse Sadler have to pacify Ken.**

It is a new morning and Sister greets Ken. In the usual way, his reply is ironic. When Sister tries to humour him, Ken engages her in the now familiar sexual banter. He tells her he wants 'to see what the old Adam' can do; she replies that she is 'a Sister not a Madame' (p. 24). Ken then implies she's a prude, and she takes the joke well before turning it back on him.

It is important to remember that Ken's innuendo should not be thought of as crude or foolish or aggressive. He is not in the position that most men are in and he therefore cannot be judged as a man in normal circumstances would be judged. His remarks ridicule no one but himself. Sister is not offended by Ken's continual teasing, but deals with her awkward patient in a calm and tolerant way that underlines her warmth and intelligence.

Adept as she is at handling Ken, Sister brings him quickly back to the point of the discussion. Ken tells her he wants to get his compensation money and asks her to contact his solicitor. Sister agrees, pleased that he appears to be planning for the distant future,

> **GLOSSARY**
>
> **the old Adam** slang for a penis. Ken suggests he might be able to have sex with Nurse Sadler, when of course this could never happen. The joke as always is on him
>
> **a Madame** a brothel keeper. Sister shows she can talk Ken's language

although this is not at all what he is doing. She tells Ken that Mrs Boyle, the medical social worker, is waiting to see him. Ken protests in a way that amuses Sister – she 'has to choke back a giggle' (p. 25) when he makes a clever dig at Dr Emerson – but he is not really in a position to resist.

Mrs Gillian Boyle, the medical social worker, now enters Ken's room. She is described in the **stage directions** as being '*very professional in her manner*' (p. 25). Although she introduces herself politely, Ken has little time for small talk and gets straight to his point. He asks her to go and tell 'Dr Frankenstein that he has successfully made his monster and he can now let it go' (p. 26). Mrs Boyle understands the implication and replies firmly that Dr Emerson is a 'first-rate physician'. She then changes the subject to the decor of the room, which she believes has improved since her last visit. Ken tells her that the room would look better still if the decorators could paint him. Unwilling to engage in polite conversation, Ken tells Mrs Boyle to get on with cheering him up. He suggests that she do a belly dance and she tells him she's forgotten her bikini. He says there is no need for one.

**CHECK THE BOOK**

In Mary Shelley's novel *Frankenstein, or The Modern Prometheus* (1818), the scientist Frankenstein creates a monster out of corpses and brings it to life.

### Resisting Mrs Boyle

Ken has been abrupt with other characters but he is consistently rude to Mrs Boyle. The problem is probably to do with the role she is obliged to play. She has no medical function. Her only task is to convince Ken to change his mind and accept the new life fate has presented him with. He requires mental toughness to resist her arguments and this leads him to dismiss everything she says. He is abrupt and dismissive but his rudeness keeps Mrs Boyle's ideas at bay and this is what he wants.

Having failed with the polite introductory talk, Mrs Boyle gets to the point. 'Dr Emerson tells me that you don't want any more treatment' (p. 26), she says. Ken thinks it is obvious why he feels like this, but Mrs Boyle observes that many of the patients she has seen in the past 'find a new way of life' (p. 27). Ken bluntly remarks that he does not want to live, a position Mrs Boyle cannot accept since she believes that it is 'the job of the hospital to save life, not to lose it' (p. 28). She then goes on to use the same line of argument as Dr Emerson, namely that Ken cannot trust his own judgement because he is depressed. She wants to give Ken therapy that will end his depression. She plans to start with a reading machine. Ken ridicules this idea. He does not want therapy because he believes his depression is entirely rational and logical. It cannot be treated.

Mrs Boyle sidesteps Ken's objections as she has done before and this makes him angry. He feels ignored and patronised. She explains that medical staff have to 'remain relatively detached' (p. 29) and this aggravates him even more. He tells her he no longer feels like a human because people such as herself will not relate to him as a human. 'The very exercise of your so-called professionalism makes me want to die' (p. 29), he says. In a distressed rage he tells Mrs Boyle to get out of his room and she leaves.

Sister goes into Ken's room and administers oxygen through a mask in order to calm Ken down. She tells Nurse Sadler to take over. When the nurse removes the mask Ken compliments Sister's shrewdness. He understands that she has cleverly sent her younger colleague in to deal with the crisis because Ken would be more tolerant of her.

> **CHECKPOINT 11**
>
> How do you think Mrs Boyle would justify her 'professional detachment'?

> **GLOSSARY**
>
> **Dr Frankenstein** the man who tried to invent an ideal human only to produce a monster. Ken implies Dr Emerson has played a similar role

Nurse Sadler asks Ken what upset him so much and he replies that it was being patronised by Mrs Boyle. When he tells Nurse Sadler that she is 'young and gentle and innocent' (p. 32), she observes that he is now patronising her. Nurse Sadler's blunt directness pleases Ken and provides a clear contrast with the detachment just shown by Mrs Boyle.

---

### Patronising Ken

Ken feels he is patronised by Mrs Boyle. He tries to communicate with her but he thinks she is not listening. This is not the case. Mrs Boyle and Dr Emerson both understand perfectly well what Ken is saying, but they cannot accept it. Nor do they want to encourage Ken in what they think is his morbidity and depression. So they gloss over his remarks or change the subject of conversation in the hope Ken will be led away from the grim view he has of his circumstances. Ken's sense of being patronised comes not from the childishness of his arguments but from their danger.

---

### PART SEVEN [pp. 32–6] – Ken talks intimately with Dr Scott

**①** Dr Scott arrives in response to Ken's distress.

**②** She advises him to accept a small dose of Valium.

**③** Ken praises Dr Scott's breasts.

**④** Ken and Dr Scott discuss his desire to die.

**CHECKPOINT 12**

What does Ken's choice of **metaphor** here tell us about the way he views his situation?

Ken apologises to Dr Scott for making a fuss over Mrs Boyle's visit. He is a little concerned that his behaviour will encourage another visit from Dr Emerson and his 'pharmaceutical truncheon' (p. 32). Dr Scott apologises for that heavy dose of Valium and advises Ken to take the tablets he is given since they won't really affect him. This is the first hint that Dr Scott is collaborating with Ken against Dr Emerson.

Dr Scott tells Ken she is pleased that he is planning to settle his compensation claim. Like the rest of her colleagues, she is heartened at the way Ken appears to be taking control of his future. This is a minor deception on Ken's part and he is probably not comfortable in practising it on Dr Scott. It may be the reason that he abruptly changes the subject to Dr Scott's physical appearance. 'You have lovely breasts' (p. 33), he says. She is, not surprisingly, caught off balance by this remark. 'I don't think it helps you to talk like this' (p. 33), she tells him. Ken thinks that the reason Dr Scott is embarrassed and surprised by his compliment is that he is no longer able to act upon his desire. This makes him pathetic, like some 'sexually desperate middle-aged man' (p. 34).

---

### Sexual banter

Ken tells Dr Scott that he now engages in 'sexual banter with young nurses, searching for the double entendre in the most innocent remark' (p. 34). He adds that 'even though I've only a piece of knotted string between my legs, I still have a man's mind'. Ken is flirtatious with Nurse Sadler and has just been directly intimate with Dr Scott. His obsessive and expressive sexuality may be the result of any or all of the following:

- His only way of getting people to listen to him is by provoking them.

- He can't stop thinking about what he has lost.

- All he has left is his mind and he will not be constrained in expressing it.

- The absurdity of his sexual condition amuses him.

- Sexual talk is the only outlet for his profound sexual frustration.

- Lying in bed all day makes him bored.

Flirtation is light-hearted. In Ken's case it masks deep and complex needs.

---

Ken now changes the conversation away from the complexities of his sexual desire. He tells Dr Scott he is serious about wanting to die. She makes the now familiar response that this is the

### GLOSSARY

**pharmaceutical truncheon** a syringe full of Valium. Ken suggests Dr Emerson's methods lack subtlety

**a piece of knotted string** a metaphor for Ken's penis. The description refers to its uselessness

**double entendre** a comment deliberately misunderstood in order to give it a sexual meaning

**CHECKPOINT 13**

Do you think Ken is right to say that his doctors are morally obliged to allow him to die?

**CHECK THE BOOK**

In *But What If She Wants To Die* you can read George Delury's diary account of his wife's battle with multiple sclerosis. She wanted to die and he assisted her suicide. Delury was sentenced to six months in jail for doing so.

consequence of a temporary depression. He replies that this does not alter the fact that he has a right to make the decision here and now. He admits the possibility that he might become happy in the future, but his **ironic** description of potential contentment suggests he does not hold out much hope. In any case, he argues, if he decides he wants to die, he must be allowed to do so. He cannot be kept artificially alive just in case he becomes content at some future date. He feels that the doctors consider their morality to be superior to his simply because they have him in their power: 'To hell with a morality that is based on the proposition that might is right' (p. 35).

Dr Scott is distressed by Ken's condition and tells him she has to leave. She does so and enters Sister's office. Sister is sympathetic to Dr Scott and tells Nurse Sadler to make a cup of tea for her. Dr Scott tells Sister that she has 'never met anyone like Mr Harrison before' (p. 35). Sister replies that a lot of the patients she has dealt with have wanted to die in just the same way as Ken. Dr Scott insists that this case is different. She says that it is not gloominess or self-pity that is leading Ken to his conclusions: 'It's just a calm rational decision' (p. 36). She reflects upon the irony of the situation that they all find themselves in. The doctors have used tremendous skills and intricate science to give Ken back his consciousness, she says. And when he uses his consciousness in ways with which they are uncomfortable, the doctors take it away again with their drugs.

**Now take a break!**

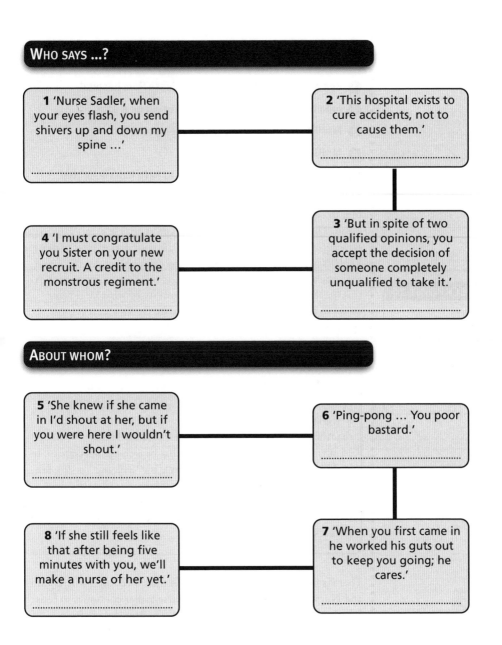

## WHO SAYS ...?

**1** 'Nurse Sadler, when your eyes flash, you send shivers up and down my spine ...'

**2** 'This hospital exists to cure accidents, not to cause them.'

**4** 'I must congratulate you Sister on your new recruit. A credit to the monstrous regiment.'

**3** 'But in spite of two qualified opinions, you accept the decision of someone completely unqualified to take it.'

## ABOUT WHOM?

**5** 'She knew if she came in I'd shout at her, but if you were here I wouldn't shout.'

**6** 'Ping-pong ... You poor bastard.'

**8** 'If she still feels like that after being five minutes with you, we'll make a nurse of her yet.'

**7** 'When you first came in he worked his guts out to keep you going; he cares.'

Check your answers on p. 88.

**PART ONE [pp. 37–46] – The law becomes involved**

1. Ken asks Mr Hill to arrange his release from hospital.

2. John tries again to get Nurse Sadler out on a date.

3. Mr Hill and Dr Emerson set out their positions.

4. Mr Hill agrees to represent Ken.

5. Dr Emerson makes arrangements to have Ken committed.

Philip Hill, Ken's solicitor, arrives at Ken's bedside. Sister has asked him to come, thinking that Ken wishes to advance his compensation claim. This is not what Ken intends to do at all. He wants Hill to get him out of the hospital so that he can die with dignity and in peace. He tells Mr Hill that he has 'coolly and calmly thought it out' and that 'each man must make his own decision' about matters such as this (p. 38). Mr Hill recognises the enormity of what he is being asked to do and tells Ken that he must see Dr Emerson before agreeing to take on the case.

**CHECKPOINT 14**

Why is it important that Ken insists on Philip Hill coming back in person to tell him whether he will accept the case?

**In control**

It is of profound importance to Ken that he maintains his possession of rationality and sound mind. If he allows himself to become at all self-pitying or depressed then he cannot be sure that the decisions he makes are the right ones. This is why he is so anxious to point out to Mr Hill that he is in mental control. It is also why he apologises to Mrs Boyle for 'whining' (p. 26). He does not want to feel sorry for himself because self-pity might cloud his judgement. Indeed, almost everything that Ken says indicates his rational and clear-headed approach to the problems he faces.

There is now another brief interlude in the sluice room where John and Nurse Sadler meet once more. Nurse Sadler continues to resist John's advances despite his persistence. The atmosphere has a relaxed and humorous intensity that suggests it will not be long before these two become more intimate. This developing intimacy serves as a reminder of the sort of life Ken has lost and the human contact he desires above all. Without those basic pleasures so easily enjoyed by John and Nurse Sadler, Ken cannot live happily.

Philip Hill now goes to see Dr Emerson in order to establish his angle on Ken's case. Mr Hill explains that Ken wishes to be discharged and Dr Emerson responds that this would have the practical effect of killing him. He considers this to be a sufficient reason for refusing Ken's request. Hill points out that such a refusal would be in direct violation of Ken's wishes. Dr Emerson argues that Ken's wishes cannot be respected since he is depressed and 'incapable of making a rational decision about his life and death' (p. 41). Mr Hill asks whether Dr Emerson would have any objection to him bringing in a psychiatrist to analyse Ken's state of mind. Dr Emerson recommends the hospital's own psychiatrist, but Hill says he would prefer to use a specialist whose opinion will be genuinely objective. The meeting ends on this rather sour note.

**EXAMINER'S SECRET**

Always consider a writer's purposes and intentions. The short scene between John and Nurse Sadler may seem irrelevant, but think about why it has been written in. What would the play lack if it was not there?

### Dr Emerson under pressure

The methods and arguments used by Dr Emerson in his meeting with Philip Hill are dubious. First he tries to pretend there is no debate since he cannot be expected to kill his patient. Nobody is asking him to do this. Then he argues that Ken's right to kill himself is rendered invalid because he is depressed and irrational. Dr Emerson has seen no evidence of this. Finally he tries to prove Ken's lack of mental balance by claiming the support of a psychiatrist who has not even examined him.

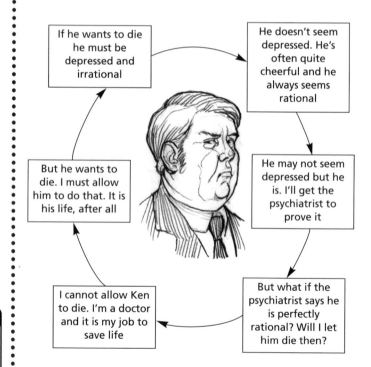

If he wants to die he must be depressed and irrational

He doesn't seem depressed. He's often quite cheerful and he always seems rational

But he wants to die. I must allow him to do that. It is his life, after all

He may not seem depressed but he is. I'll get the psychiatrist to prove it

I cannot allow Ken to die. I'm a doctor and it is my job to save life

But what if the psychiatrist says he is perfectly rational? Will I let him die then?

### CHECKPOINT 15

At what point in the diagram can you see the weakness in Dr Emerson's logic? How do you think he would defend his reasoning?

Philip Hill returns to Ken's bedside and gives him an outline of the discussion he has just had with Dr Emerson. He explains that Dr Emerson is likely to have Ken detained at the hospital under the provisions of the Mental Health Act. This means that Ken will be given treatment against his wishes on the basis that his opinions are unsound. It now becomes more crucial than ever, therefore, for Ken to convince the psychiatrists that he is sane. If he cannot do so he will become the hospital's prisoner.

Dr Emerson calls upon the hospital's psychiatrist, Dr Paul Travers, to explain how he can use the Mental Health Act to detain Ken against his will in hospital. Dr Travers explains that two signatures are required, only one of which can come from the patient's own hospital. He adds that getting a second signature from an external psychiatrist should not be a problem so long as there is no doubt about Ken's clinical depression. Dr Emerson is a little impatient with this: 'You haven't understood. He's suicidal. He's determined to kill himself' (p. 44). Dr Travers points out that there are psychiatrists who would not take suicidal tendencies as evidence of insanity. He agrees, however, to find someone who is likely to share Dr Emerson's view of the case. Dr Emerson is relieved to find some support. 'I'm very grateful', he tells Dr Travers as he leaves, 'and Harrison will be too' (p. 45).

## Means and ends

Dr Emerson asks Dr Travers to find an external psychiatrist 'who believes in something better than suicide' (p. 44). In doing this he is trying to load the dice in favour of an insanity judgement against Ken. Dr Travers says he knows of 'a chap at Ellertree ... a very staunch Catholic, I believe. Would that suit you?' (p. 44). The two of them are conniving in order to produce the outcome Dr Emerson wants. This is justified, Dr Emerson feels, because he is certain he is right. The underhand means are needed to reach his desired ends.

Dr Emerson updates Dr Scott on recent events. She is unsurprised to discover that Ken has decided to discharge himself and she

**GLOSSARY**

**a very staunch Catholic** members of this Christian body are strongly opposed to suicide. This particular psychiatrist's response to Ken's position can therefore be safely predicted in advance questions whether Dr Emerson is right to use legal means to detain him against his will. Dr Emerson stresses that he is the one obliged to take responsibility over Ken's life and death. He refuses to believe that someone as intelligent as Ken could choose to die and takes the fact that he has done so as evidence of insanity. Dr Scott points out that the decision to die is not necessarily the act of an unbalanced mind. Dr Emerson replies that 'a doctor cannot accept the choice for death; he's committed to life' (p. 46). Dr Scott believes that her senior colleague is behaving not like a doctor but like a judge. Dr Emerson responds by warning Dr Scott that should Ken die unexpectedly he will be suspicious. The two of them have defined their positions and now disagree with one another openly and completely.

---

**CHECKPOINT 16**

How might fear explain Dr Emerson's behaviour?

---

### Doctor or judge?

Dr Emerson says, 'I'm a doctor, not a judge' (p. 46). Is this true?

Dr Emerson's first principle is that patients must be kept alive. All else follows from this. It is a fine conviction for a doctor to have. But Dr Emerson is too much the perfect doctor. He will not accept that occasionally exceptions will occur that should lead him temporarily to suspend his rules. So Dr Emerson is both a doctor and a judge. By being too principled a doctor he becomes a terrible judge, imprisoning Ken in a life which is a nightmare to him.

---

### PART TWO [pp. 46–51] – Ken is visited by Dr Travers

**1** Ken speaks fluently with Dr Travers.

**2** Dr Travers remains unconvinced about Ken's sanity.

Ken greets Dr Travers in his usual, **ironic** manner. He asks whether Dr Travers is on his side and remarks that this may sound paranoid. Dr Travers takes this as a cue for discussion and asks Ken to define paranoia. Ken feels it is the need always to be right and the matching fear of ever being wrong. If he were to display these symptoms he would be called paranoid. He suggests that in the case of Dr Emerson and others like him this inflexibility of mind is viewed as a strength.

Ken's dig at Dr Emerson provides Dr Travers with another cue to examine his patient's state of mind. He asks what is wrong with doctors. Ken says that in general terms they are too authoritarian. They make decisions for their patients without reference to them. Dr Travers responds to this claim in a way already demonstrated by Dr Emerson. He says that doctors have medical knowledge and training that endows them with the authority to make decisions their patients cannot understand. Ken feels that the circumstances in which patients cannot be helped to understand are rare. He says that once the doctor has provided all the relevant information it is up to the patient alone to make the necessary decisions. In his own case, Ken concludes, he has decided to die.

Dr Travers, confronted with this hard fact, tells Ken that his intelligence weakens his case. Ken counters that this 'sounds like Catch 22. If you're clever and sane enough to put up an invincible case for suicide, it demonstrates you ought not to die' (pp. 48–9).

Ken makes a joke about Dr Travers moving his chair. Dr Travers responds well but does the usual 'professional' thing and refuses to engage with Ken on an equal and personal level. He quickly returns the conversation to Ken, asking him about his personal life. Ken tells him that fortunately he is not married. He did have a fiancée, whom he told not to visit him any more. He made this decision, he says, in order to release her 'from the guilt she would feel if she did what she really wanted to' (p. 49). Ken assumes that what she really wants is another man and he does not want her to feel bad about getting one. Dr Travers remarks that this is an act of great generosity on Ken's part. Ken does not feel it is. He says that he made the decision so that he could retain his self-respect. He does not want to be the object of other people's pity. Ken goes on to speak about his parents and their reaction to his plight. He admires the unexpected strength demonstrated by his mother.

Dr Travers's conclusion from this lengthy interview with Ken is that 'we shall have to see … I shall have to do some tests' (p. 50). Ken is understandably infuriated by this response but tries to contain his anger so that the psychiatrist will not write him off 'as in a manic phase of a manic depressive cycle' (p. 50). He tells Dr Travers not to visit him again as it will make him more and more depressed and 'eventually you will have destroyed my mind' (p. 51).

---

**CHECKPOINT 17**

What would you be thinking at this stage if you were Dr Travers?

---

### Sanity

'Can anyone prove that they are sane?' Ken asks Dr Travers. 'Could you?' (p. 51).

Throughout this interview Ken demonstrates both his intellect and his emotional intelligence. He engages with Dr Travers as an equal. He shows an awareness of his own predicament, acutely aware that any statement he makes could cause this psychiatrist to pin a psychosis (severe mental disorder) on him. He avoids this trap by standing apart from his condition, talking about himself in a detached and objective fashion. The comments he makes concerning his personal life show him to be both compassionate and realistic. It is hard to imagine anyone in Ken's position making a better case for his own sanity.

## PART THREE [pp. 51–5] – Mr Hill and Dr Scott confirm their support for Ken

**❶ Philip Hill and Dr Scott return from dinner.**

**❷ Ken is fed by Nurse Sadler.**

**❸ Ken feels more alive but still wants to die.**

The action of the play now moves forward to the evening. Philip Hill and Dr Scott return to the hospital from a meal in a restaurant and are discussing Ken's case. Dr Scott feels they are considering something very near to euthanasia. Mr Hill argues that it is not euthanasia but suicide. He gets Dr Scott to accept that were Ken to have the use of his arms 'for just one minute' she would assist him in killing himself (p. 51). It follows for Mr Hill that those who sympathise with Ken should be prepared to act as his arms and help him to die. Part of the problem, he feels, is that suicide is seen as some sort of failure. Mr Hill feels that it would be far better to say that nothing and no one is to blame if a patient is facing impossible circumstances and chooses to die.

**DID YOU KNOW?**

Euthanasia translates literally from ancient Greek as 'good death'. It is used nowadays to refer to the act of painlessly but deliberately causing the death of someone who is suffering from an incurable condition. It is often referred to as mercy killing.

**DID YOU KNOW?**

Euthanasia was legalised in the Netherlands and Belgium in 2002.

### GLOSSARY

**in a manic phase of a manic depressive cycle** a severe mental illness in which a patient alternates between hysteria and depression. Ken's ability to view himself as others (could) see him is strong evidence that he is not insane

**CHECKPOINT 18**

How do you think
Dr Emerson would
react if one of his
patients committed
suicide?

## Euthanasia or suicide

Dr Scott fears she may be about to condone euthanasia, sometimes known as 'mercy killing'. This is the act of ending the life of someone who is suffering. Suicide, on the other hand, is the act of ending one's own life. Euthanasia is a more difficult ethical problem since it actually involves one person physically ending the life of another. Dr Scott would feel uncomfortable going this far. Mr Hill assures her, however, that she is not being asked to do this since the removal of care is not an active form of ending someone else's life. Ken has taken his own decisions and his death would be suicide.

Dr Scott and Philip Hill part on friendly and potentially intimate terms. The scene returns to Ken's room, where Nurse Sadler arrives with the evening meal. She feeds it to Ken with a spoon and gives him water from a cup. He **parodies** the occasion, pretending to be enjoying a meal in an exclusive restaurant. Then he laughs at his own failure to recognise the brand of sterilising fluid in the drinking water. He imagines the hospital staff activating emergency procedures in order to revive his taste buds. Nurse Sadler leaves when he refuses any more food.

## Parody

A parody is a mocking contrast. Ken parodies his eating arrangements by portraying them as dignified and refined when clearly they are not. He wants to draw attention to his state of childlike dependence by doing so. He then parodies the hospital's emergency procedures in order to demonstrate how pointless they have turned out to be in his case. On a deeper level too, this whole scene is a parody since it contrasts with the meal just enjoyed by Dr Scott and Philip Hill. It highlights the difference between the life Ken lives and the life he would otherwise wish to have.

Dr Scott enters Ken's room. Ken asks her where she has been and she tells him. He is amused and envious at the news she has been out with Mr Hill. There is no longer any 'professional' breeziness about her manner and Ken has dropped his **ironic** digs. There is a sense that these two are now friends who understand and respect each other. Ken seems to have achieved at least a part of what he wanted. He is being treated without pity as an adult and an equal. He concedes that for the first time since the accident he feels 'like a human being again' (p. 55). This is not enough, however. He will never have the life he wants and he wishes still to die.

> **CHECKPOINT 19**
> We know that Ken finds both Nurse Sadler and Dr Scott attractive. Does he respond to the two of them in the same way?

### PART FOUR [pp. 56–60] – Ken is visited by his legal team

**❶ Philip Hill and Peter Kershaw visit Ken.**

**❷ The legal options are outlined.**

Philip Hill arrives in the hospital corridor with Ken's barrister, Peter Kershaw. Mr Hill confirms that Ken seems sane and that the hospital is holding him under the terms of the Mental Health Act. The two of them share what they think is a private joke about Sister before they greet her in her office.

Sister tells them that Dr Emerson has insisted a member of hospital staff be present during interviews with Ken. A sense of mutual suspicion between the two sides is perceptible. Mr Kershaw has little choice but to accept Sister's terms.

The three of them go into Ken's room and Mr Hill explains that Sister is present 'to see you don't get too excited' (p. 57). This amuses Ken, who says he cannot help but get excited by her. He then pretends to misunderstand what she is doing when she takes back the bedcovers and reaches for his pulse. Ken's sexual play-acting is affectionate. Sister is working hard to keep Ken alive and he does not resent her for this. Their fondness for one another reflects well on them both.

Mr Kershaw now explains to Ken the medical consequences of his proposed actions. If he leaves the hospital he will be dead within a week. Ken acknowledges that he understands the situation and is eager to pursue his case. Mr Kershaw is relieved at Ken's reassurance and outlines the procedures they have open to them. One of them is to 'appeal to a tribunal', but this could take as long as a year. Ken is horrified at this. 'I really would be crazy in a year', he says (p. 59).

**CHECKPOINT 20**

Would it prove anyone right if Ken did go insane?

### Driving Ken mad

Ken frequently expresses fears about what life in the hospital is doing to him. He tells Mrs Boyle that her professionalism makes him want to die, and he accuses Dr Travers of trying to destroy his mind. Now he is terrified that if a tribunal takes a year to hear his case he will go mad. Ken must prove his sanity and he must do it quickly. Otherwise he may well lose his mind and be unable to argue for the death he so desperately wants.

Mr Hill suggests that instead of using a tribunal they try habeas corpus, and Kershaw explains to Ken what 'a writ of habeas corpus' is (p. 59). Under this procedure, Ken would have the chance to prove that the hospital was keeping him a prisoner with no good cause. The hearing would probably have to be before a judge in

Ken's room at the hospital. Ken agrees with his legal team that this is the best option, and his two advisers leave. On the way out, Mr Hill offers Sister his sympathies. She overheard his earlier remark to Mr Kershaw (p. 56) about her 'stainless steel heart' and tells him sardonically that it's therefore 'easy to keep it sterilised of emotion' (p. 60).

---

### A stainless steel heart?

Philip Hill comes out of this little exchange looking something like a shabby hypocrite. Sister emerges as sharp, witty and wronged. It is another reminder that we must not judge these characters solely by the side they are on in the discussion about Ken's life. This is a serious play that does not pretend people are simply good or bad according to their stated positions in a debate.

---

## PART FIVE [pp. 61–6] – The morning of the judgement

**❶ Ken has a friendly chat with Nurse Sadler and John.**

**❷ There are brief visits from Dr Scott and Dr Emerson.**

**❸ Dr Emerson and Philip Hill discuss issues raised by the case.**

The action now moves on to the morning of the legal hearing. Nurse Sadler and John are in the process of preparing Ken's room. John absent-mindedly starts to sing a song called 'Dry Bones' for which Nurse Sadler ticks him off. She feels it is an insensitive thing to do in Ken's presence. Ken is far more interested in the familiar way Nurse Sadler has spoken to John and he mentions this. John admits that he adores Nurse Sadler, and she quickly sends him out of the room to get a chair. It emerges that Nurse Sadler and John have been out the previous evening to a club where John plays in a band. Ken says that John often cheers him up when he is miserable because he is unafraid to make jokes about his physical condition. Ken believes that the guilt felt by other members of the hospital staff stops them from sharing the details of their lives with him. They do not want him to feel he is missing out on anything.

**GLOSSARY**

**tribunal** a group of experts appointed to resolve some disagreement

**a writ of habeas corpus** issued to release someone being held unjustly. These writs are now uncommon because police in the UK are no longer allowed to hold suspects for an unspecified length of time. Habeas corpus is Latin for 'you may have the body'.

## CHECKPOINT 21

In what ways does Ken feel Nurse Sadler has demonstrated guilt during the course of his conversation with her?

### A harsh judgement?

A more tolerant man than Ken might interpret his carers' 'guilt' (p. 62) as sensitivity. After all, not every sick person wishes to hear about all the good things open to the healthy. He might also have more understanding of the need for professionalism amongst the staff. It would not be appropriate for doctors to chatter on about their sex lives to patients. Time and again, however, we have seen that Ken cannot think generously of those who do not speak openly with him, whatever their reasons.

John returns carrying Sister's armchair for the judge to sit in. He sits in it himself, thereby demonstrating a playful disregard for the authority of both Sister and the judge. The irreverent tone continues when John starts to **parody** the hearing about to take place. His humour is in stark dramatic contrast to the events about to unfold.

Sister arrives and the play-acting stops. The serious drama is about to begin. For once, Ken seems awkward and a little tongue-tied. He is uncomfortable in Sister's presence because in all conscience he knows she has done her best for him. Now he is going to attempt to kill himself, thereby bringing all her efforts to nothing. He tells her he feels 'a bit like a traitor' (p. 63). She replies politely but without warmth and then leaves.

## CHECKPOINT 22

How do you feel about Sister's reaction to Ken on the morning of the hearing?

Dr Scott now comes in and Ken relaxes. He knows that she understands and sympathises with his position in a way that Sister cannot bring herself to do. Dr Scott asks Ken one final time if he wishes to go ahead with his plans and Ken confirms that he does. Ken tells her he has had no mind-altering medication for two days and Dr Scott reveals that this is on the judge's orders. This is an early indication that this judge is genuinely eager to get to the truth of Ken's case. Dr Emerson then joins Ken and Dr Scott. He tells Ken that it is not too late to change his mind. Ken will not change his position, however, and nor will Dr Emerson. Dr Emerson leaves the room and Dr Scott tells Ken: 'If I didn't know *you* I'd say *he* was the most obstinate man I've ever met' (p. 65).

### Dr Emerson's view

As he leaves the bedside, Dr Emerson tells Ken: 'I wish you the best of luck Mr Harrison, so that we'll be able to carry on treating you' (p. 65). He means that it is in Ken's best interests not to get what he wants. Dr Emerson believes that, like young children and the insane, Ken is better off if the important decisions are taken for him.

As he walks down the corridor away from Ken's room, Dr Emerson is greeted by Philip Hill. They exchange a few terse words about the case. Dr Emerson is confident that Ken's application will be turned down, because the law will not, as he puts it, 'force me to watch a patient of mine die unnecessarily' (p. 65). He believes that the law will not intervene in an issue he considers best left to the professionals involved. Mr Hill disagrees. He says it is the duty of the law to intervene whenever anyone, professional or otherwise, seems to be exercising 'arbitrary power' over anyone else.

### Pride

Dr Emerson takes great pride in doing his job well, and this is one of the things that make him a good doctor. His pride, however, seems to be getting in the way of his judgement. Even at this stage of the debate he still insists on talking about the issue as if it were primarily about himself. At no point in the discussion with Mr Hill does he mention Ken's needs or his self-evident ability to take decisions for himself. Dr Emerson concentrates instead upon how the case affects his authority as a doctor. His greatest concern is not for Ken's well-being but with the potential threat to his own influence.

**DID YOU KNOW?**
Living wills were introduced into the United Kingdom by the Voluntary Euthanasia Society during the 1980s. They allow people to state what they wish to happen to them should they lose their faculties.

**GLOSSARY**
**arbitrary power** power that no one has the right to question. Dr Emerson feels he has earned the right to act according to his professional judgement. Mr Hill says he can make such judgements but they must never be the final word

## PART SIX [pp. 67–71] – The hearing

**1** Dr Emerson states his case to Judge Millhouse.

**2** Dr Barr argues Ken's case to the judge.

The hearing begins. Judge Millhouse starts by describing how it will proceed. He says that first he will hear Dr Emerson outline the reasons why he is detaining Ken. Then he will hear Dr Barr, a consultant psychiatrist from a different hospital, explain why he thinks Ken is sane and should be released. If there is any doubt remaining after these two specialists have made their representations, then Judge Millhouse will question Ken himself. The witnesses, Dr Emerson and Dr Barr, will be questioned by Ken's barrister, Peter Kershaw; and the hospital's barrister, Andrew Eden.

Dr Emerson is the first to speak. He gives a detailed explanation of Ken's physical injuries then goes on to argue that Ken is of unsound mind. It is impossible, says Dr Emerson, for a person to have had an accident like Ken's and not to have been affected mentally. He believes that people like Ken can go on making 'wrong decisions' (p. 68) for months and years after an accident. He does not think that Ken's depression is justified by his circumstances. He thinks that it is a medical illness that can be treated. He concedes that there is no objective way he can prove his opinion but thinks that his experience as a doctor should be sufficient to reassure doubters.

---

**Catch 22**

Dr Emerson's submission to Judge Millhouse allows no way out for Ken. If Ken agrees with Dr Emerson, he will have proved his sanity and his right to choose life. If he disagrees, he has demonstrated insanity and has no right to choose death. Either way, agree or disagree, Ken must stay alive. Dr Emerson has created the perfect 'Catch 22' (see Act II, p. 48).

---

Dr Barr now takes the oath. He is the witness called by Ken's legal team in support of the application for the writ of habeas corpus. Dr Barr describes how he has examined Ken and come to the conclusion that 'he is reacting in a perfectly rational way to a very bad situation' (p. 70). He says, like Dr Emerson before him, that there are no objective tests that can prove his point. He concedes that his judgements are based solely on his experience as a practitioner dealing with many similar cases. Dr Barr concludes that although Ken is of sound mind he disagrees with the decision he has made.

There are two key points to remember from Dr Barr's statement. First, it demonstrates that there may be disagreement amongst professionals over the diagnosis of their patients. Dr Emerson often relies on 'professional opinion' as if it always comes to the same conclusions and is questioned only by the ignorant. Dr Barr shows that this is not the case. His testimony is evidence that a professional psychiatrist does not necessarily view depression as evidence of illness or unsound mind. The second important thing to notice is Dr Barr's open disagreement with Ken's decision to die. Although he apologises to Ken for revealing this sentiment, it actually strengthens Ken's case. The point is this: Dr Barr, like Dr Emerson, thinks Ken is wrong to want to die. Dr Barr, however, respects Ken's right to make that decision and considers him perfectly competent to do so.

**DID YOU KNOW?**

A psychiatrist is a doctor of the brain who can treat mental illness with drugs in the same way that other doctors treat physical ailments.

The submission of evidence to the judge is therefore inconclusive. Dr Emerson and Dr Barr have both relied on their own experience as doctors to come to opposite conclusions. Dr Emerson's experience leads him to conclude that Ken is of unsound mind and must not be allowed to make important decisions. Dr Barr's experience brings him to the conclusion that Ken is depressed but sane and should be allowed to take decisions even if they are disagreeable to others. Judge Millhouse must therefore question Ken himself to come to the crucial and final judgement: is Ken sane?

## PART SEVEN [pp. 71–6] – The decision

❶ Judge Millhouse questions Ken.

❷ The application is granted.

❸ Ken agrees to remain at the hospital until his death.

Judge Millhouse is now solely responsible for making a decision on Ken's state of mind. Ken is pessimistic at first. He thinks that the judge is 'too kind' (p. 71), too warm-hearted to make a decision that will result in Ken's death.

Judge Millhouse begins by asking Ken why Dr Emerson thinks he is incapable of rational thought. Ken's reply is both rational and generous even to a fault. He says that Dr Emerson is wrong but for the right reasons. Dr Emerson is a good man and an excellent professional. He will not let a patient die if he can help it. The judge then draws the distinction between a sane depression and a medical depression. Ken says that this matter has already been dealt with by his own psychiatrist, who has pronounced him sane.

Judge Millhouse asks Ken why he wants to die. Ken replies that he does not want to die, but nor does he 'wish to live at any price' (p. 72). This is another one of those fine distinctions that show Ken's mind to be functioning extremely well. What Ken is pointing out here is that he is not suicidal at all. He has no desire to die. But if he cannot live in the way he wishes to live then the hospital is committing 'an act of deliberate cruelty' (p. 73) by keeping him alive.

---

**CHECKPOINT 24**

How would you describe the conversation between Judge Millhouse and Ken?

---

The final part of Ken's argument is centred on the importance of choice. He tells Judge Millhouse that some people should be allowed to die and some should be kept alive. It is cruel to keep those alive who wish to die and equally cruel to let those die who wish to live. Many people with terrible handicaps live dignified and rewarding lives, 'but the dignity starts with ... choice' (p. 74). Ken has chosen not to continue living and to force life on him is, in his own words, undignified, appalling and inhumane.

Having listened to Ken's reasonable and well-considered arguments, Judge Millhouse sums up the case in a lengthy **monologue**. He says that Dr Emerson's position on suicide is unsustainable. Many people have made a 'deliberate decision to embark on a course of action that will lead inevitably to death' (p. 74), in war, most obviously, and they are considered heroes not insane. The issue for the judge is whether or not Ken is mad. He says that many people he has seen in the witness box appear quite sane but behave at other times in ways that demonstrate they are not. If Ken is making an excellent job of disguising his insanity then his appeals must be ignored. The judge, however, is satisfied that Ken is perfectly sane and therefore should not be held against his will for his own good by the hospital. He grants the writ of habeas corpus and instructs Dr Emerson to release his patient.

Judge Millhouse leaves and Ken is left for a few moments with Dr Scott and Dr Emerson. Ken says he will leave the hospital but Dr Emerson asks him to stay. He tells Ken that his life-support systems will be removed and he will be dead within a week. Ken thanks Dr Emerson for this generous-spirited act. Dr Emerson replies that he is doing it so that should Ken change his mind he can be resuscitated.

Dr Emerson leaves and Ken is left alone with Dr Scott. She stands to go and then moves towards Ken as if to kiss him. He thanks her for the thought but tells her to leave, which she does. Ken is left alone and the play comes to an end.

**CHECKPOINT 25**

What do you make of Dr Emerson's motives in inviting Ken to stay on in his room?

 **DID YOU KNOW?**

In England and Wales, assisting a suicide carries a prison term of up to fourteen years.

**CHECK THE BOOK**

*The Right to Die* by Elaine Landau is a short examination of the euthanasia and assisted-suicide debate written specifically for students.

**Now take a break!**

## Who says ...?

**1** 'I'm not asking that you make any decision about my life and death, merely that you represent me and my views to the hospital.'

..................................................

**2** 'Try and find an old codger like me, who believes in something better than suicide.'

..................................................

**4** 'I'm not saying that you would find life easy but you do have resources that an unintelligent person doesn't have.'

..................................................

**3** 'A man might want to die for perfectly sane reasons.'

..................................................

## About whom?

**5** 'The randy old devil. He didn't take long to get cracking did he?'

..................................................

**6** 'Here is my substitute mum, with her porcelain pap.'

..................................................

**8** 'He's sorry for me but knows bloody well it isn't his fault. He's a tonic.'

..................................................

**7** 'Is she your standard gorgon?'

..................................................

Check your answers on p. 88.

## PART THREE

## COMMENTARY

### THEMES

#### IMPRISONMENT, HUMILIATION AND LOSS OF AUTONOMY

**DID YOU KNOW?**

Despite being unable to speak or write except through a computer, Stephen Hawking has produced scientific papers as well as several bestselling science books, including the popular *A Brief History of Time*.

**EXAMINER'S SECRET**

Consider how scenes from the play might affect you if you were really watching it. This will help you write more eloquently about the play's dramatic impact.

Ken Harrison spends the entire play trapped in a hospital bed. This fact is obvious to an audience actually watching the play, but it is easy to forget as a student who may only have had the chance to read it. Ken is imprisoned by the injuries resulting from his car accident. He is not the kind of person who, like Stephen Hawking (see **Setting and background**), can gain important freedom from mental activity alone. Nor is he the sort of patient who would gain satisfaction from learning to do things like turning 'the pages of a book with some miracle of modern science' (Act I, p. 34). Ken has been an active man, a sculptor whose life and work depended on his delicate skills. Once these capabilities have disappeared he is trapped without purpose or direction or hope. Ken's hopelessness is made worse by the fact that his body continues to function at its most basic levels. He is subject to regular medical processes involving the control, his body's waste products, processes which, whilst necessary to keep him alive, are utterly humiliating.

Perhaps the worst consequence of Ken's imprisonment, however, is his loss of autonomy. All prisoners suffer some degree of this, even those kept in open prisons. Ken, however, has less influence over his own future than the most dangerous prisoners in the highest-security jails. He cannot decide on his own to do anything at all. He cannot resist Dr Emerson with his needle of Valium. He cannot even decide to die. In these circumstances it is hardly surprising that Ken views death as a form of liberation. Given the terrible nature of his imprisonment it is fitting that the process that does eventually free him is normally associated with prisoners of the law rather than patients of a hospital.

#### SANITY AND DEPRESSION

Ken's 'imprisonment' is justified by the belief that he is 'mentally unbalanced' (Act II, p. 41). When others think you are mad (or want to think you are mad) it may be impossible to persuade them otherwise. Anything you say or do can be taken as evidence of madness. This is why Ken is so desperate to act normally during his interview with Dr Travers. The problem gets worse if depression is involved, because most people feel that depression should be cured. Ken needs to prove to others that a depression need not be clinical (without proper cause) but sane. A sane depression is a rational response to real circumstances and should not be used as evidence of madness.

## AUTHORITY, MORALITY AND CHOICE

Ken says at one point to Dr Scott: 'To hell with a morality that is based on the proposition that might is right' (Act I, p. 35). Ken is thinking about Dr Emerson's belief in life over death. This moral view holds that suicide or assisted suicide can never be the right thing to do. It asserts that with the correct help, and with effective palliative care, all patients can lead full and relatively painless lives. Ken, needless to say, does not believe this. He thinks that sane and rational patients should have absolute authority over their futures, including the choice between life and death. They are, in Ken's view, in a better position to judge. If people like Emerson became paralysed, their high moral tone might change. Until his legal victory, though, it is not Ken but the hospital and its agents who make decisions about Ken's future. They have authority and what they consider to be morally superior arguments. According to Ken, however, they can only impose these judgements because of his weakness. In other words, their 'might' or their power means that the choices they make are viewed as the right ones, whereas his are ignored.

## DUTY AND RESPONSIBILITY

It is good to be dutiful and responsible, or at least it is good up to a point. Characters like Dr Emerson carry the concept of duty too far. It becomes the only thing of importance and prevents them from working for the general benefit. Those whose only concern is to perform their duty can end up being satisfied with their work even if they cause avoidable misery.

**DID YOU KNOW?**
The practice of 'death tourism' is growing rapidly in the UK. It involves travelling overseas to countries where assisted dying is legal.

## PROFESSIONALISM AND CARE

Many of the hospital staff depicted in the play are highly professional, and they are the ones Ken likes least. He believes that professionalism is a way of keeping patients at arm's length. The medical personnel who demonstrate professionalism are brisk and optimistic and businesslike. In reality, they have little time for patients like Ken who demonstrate repeatedly a desire for intelligent conversation and who raise difficult and thought-provoking questions. Questions about the futures of seriously ill patients do not fit in with the bustling attitudes of professionals such as Dr Emerson, and they cleverly avoid them. Consequently, Ken feels patronised and then infuriated. This is why the real care, from Ken's point of view, comes from those who are least professional. In this play, care is about shared humanity, not professional excellence.

Ken might be considered to be slightly unfair in his description of those set in opposition to him. He rarely, if ever, acknowledges that the professionalism he despises is necessary on one level for the smooth and proper functioning of an efficient hospital. Perhaps there is a balance to be struck between professional duty and the individual care and attention required and requested by patients such as Ken.

## HUMANITY AND SEXUALITY

Ken is, or at least was, a physical person. His work as a sculptor was to do with his hands. He cannot envisage a life where he is simply a brain. His humanity is tied up with his body, and his body is symbolised by his sexuality. Ken wishes to communicate with the women around him in a way that is both physical and emotional. The emotional side he can still manage very well, as his relationships with Dr Scott and Nurse Sadler suggest. The physical side is to him a joke at best. The idea, therefore, is that a human being's physical needs are tied to his or her emotional needs. Brian Clark suggests that if physical needs (in Ken's case, his sexual yearnings) are frustrated, then an essential part of humanity disappears. Ken himself accepts that not all patients in his condition would feel this way, but it is something that affects Ken's character powerfully.

## IDENTITY AND CHILDHOOD

Ken feels he has lost his identity and become little more than a baby. 'Here is my substitute mum, with her porcelain pap', he says of Nurse Sadler. 'This isn't for me' (Act II, p. 55). Childhood is characterised most of all by dependency and Ken is utterly dependent on others. All he really has left is his sharp mind, and this is often ignored. Ken detests his regression to a state of childhood and the loss of his adult identity. Stimulating conversation with Dr Scott is a help to him (it reminds him he is an adult), but in the end it is not enough. Here again there is the distinction to be drawn between real-life characters in a state of dependence, and Ken. We know of those who are physically dependent but whose contribution to society through their ideas or force of character is enormous. Ken's experience, however, is different: he finds it very difficult to retain his sense of adulthood.

## THE PROBLEM OF MEDICATION

Drugs are of tremendous benefit to society. The development of medication in the last hundred years has meant that much terrible pain and suffering has disappeared from a great part of human experience. We only have to look at news pictures from those parts of the world where there are shortages of drugs to see how desperate life can be without them. Despite that, Ken's experience reminds us that there are two sides to this. Medication has kept him alive, it is true, but it also prolongs his life and dulls his mind against his will. The play suggests that scientific knowledge must be combined with sensitivity towards those it is designed to benefit.

# STRUCTURE

## FIRST DAY

The play begins in the morning. Ken is visited in turn by Sister Anderson, Nurse Sadler, John, Dr Scott and Dr Emerson. The atmosphere is light, though there is an undercurrent of dissatisfaction in Ken's tone. Dr Scott picks up on this and decides to prescribe Valium, which Ken then persuades her not to administer. The action is intense (it all takes place in this single

**CHECK THE NET**
There are many organisations that have been formed over the last decades to promote both sides of the euthanasia debate. Type 'euthanasia' into your search engine and see what organisations come up.

morning, one event after another) and is centred on Ken's room. This use of time and location is claustrophobic and quickly identifies Ken as the recipient of a rather too intensive care.

The action then moves to the sluice room later on in the day, where John is attempting to seduce a half-amused Nurse Sadler. The location contrasts with the sterility of other places in the hospital, and this switch in scene offers the audience and reader a moment of light relief. Time has passed and the intensity of the morning's activity is replaced with a more relaxed and human feel.

Later in the day, the play regains its intensity. Dr Scott is trying to persuade Dr Emerson that her decision not to give Ken the Valium was the right one. Emerson disagrees and takes the Valium himself to Ken's room, where he forcibly injects him. The location is very important here. The decisions are made in Dr Emerson's office and they are implemented in Ken's room without Ken's consent. Power descends on Ken from outside and then disappears having exercised its will. No wonder Ken compares the consultants to the gods.

The first day ends outside Ken's room in Sister's office. The nurses chat with Dr Scott and then say goodnight. Again, away from the claustrophobia of the sickroom, the atmosphere is more relaxed; but there is a sense of an impending storm.

## SECOND DAY

The second day of action follows on immediately from the first. Events begin again in the morning with Ken chatting to Sister and Nurse Sadler. Things quickly take a turn for the worse when Mrs Boyle comes to visit. She infuriates Ken with her professional coolness. When she has left, Ken is calmed by the visits of Sister, Nurse Sadler and Dr Scott. With the focus firmly on his room, Ken is again the weakened centre of attention. This attention can create distress or pleasure but whichever it causes it is usually intense. As with the action on the first morning, visitors follow quickly, one after another. Ken lies in bed and people appear. He must receive them all; he cannot pretend to be out or leave the phone unanswered. All he has to oppose or match his guests is his mental sharpness. There is no gap in time, no relief. This relentless structure

**DID YOU KNOW?**

Brian Clark originally wrote *Whose Life is it Anyway?* for television. Do you think the play would work better on television or on stage?

creates a sense of the pressure on Ken. The morning ends with him falling asleep, exhausted.

## THIRD DAY

The action on the third day of the play takes place some time after the events of the first two days. Ken's solicitor, Philip Hill, has been contacted and arrives to discuss his case.

He has an argument with Dr Emerson about Ken's circumstances. Dr Emerson then discusses the case with Dr Travers and Dr Scott. These events take place in Dr Emerson's office, reinforcing the impression that it is here, and not Ken's room, where the important decisions are made. Light relief is provided by John's continued comic pursuit of Nurse Sadler in the sluice room.

Later in the day, Dr Travers visits Ken. He refuses to recognise Ken's obvious sanity because of the problems in doing so. This is an important moment in the play and it stands apart from other events in time.

The third day ends late at night. Dr Scott and Philip Hill return from a meal and say goodnight in the street. The everyday freedom of being outside contrasts with Ken's confinement in his hospital room.

## FOURTH DAY

Enough time now passes for Philip Hill to have arranged for a barrister, Peter Kershaw, to represent Ken. Mr Hill and Mr Kershaw visit Ken and discuss his options with him. They agree to apply for a writ of habeas corpus. Slowly, Ken's room is changing from being the place where decisions are implemented to one where decisions are made.

## FIFTH DAY

Again there has been a passage of time. The gap between the events of the fifth day and those of the fourth has been long enough for both sides to prepare their cases and for a judge to be appointed. The action of the day begins with John and Nurse Sadler. Events

**CHECK THE BOOK**

In *Let Me Die Before I Wake*, Derek Humphry assembles the real-life stories of terminally ill people who have practised the rational suicide Ken desires.

quickly become more serious with the arrival of the legal representatives and Judge Millhouse. Ken's case is heard. This long final scene is witnessed by the audience as it is witnessed by the characters: in real time. Ken's room is transformed from a personal space into a public one. It is no longer the stage on which Dr Emerson fulfils his duty but the place in which Ken asserts his most basic rights. When the judge makes his decision to free Ken, Dr Emerson invites Ken to stay in the room to die. Ken is finally the undisputed master of his own space.

## CHARACTERS

### KEN HARRISON

In an important sense, Ken's character is what the entire play is about. It is Ken's refusal to accept his fate, his insistence on his rights, that provides the motivating force behind virtually every event that takes place.

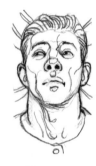

**Intelligent**
**Depressed**
**Resourceful**
**Determined**

Ken is a tremendously strong-minded individual. He lies in his bed all day, often alone, yet he retains a sense of his own needs which he expresses clearly even in the face of stubborn opposition. Foremost amongst these is his desire to die: or, more accurately, his refusal to go on living in his helpless state. He asserts this need repeatedly and convincingly until it is recognised by those with the authority to fulfil it. Without his single-minded application, Ken would degenerate into complete dependency.

Underlying his extraordinary level of application is an impressive intellect. In all his serious conversations – with Dr Scott, Dr Emerson, Dr Travers, Judge Millhouse – Ken demonstrates that he has a full grasp of all the issues affecting his case. He is able to develop an argument at length or provide sharp rejoinders to points with which he disagrees. His obvious intelligence makes a nonsense of the hospital's claim that he is mentally unsound.

Ken is also a very human person. We can sympathise wholly with his needs as he lies paralysed – yet never self-pitying – in his hospital bed. He takes pleasure in the development of John's relationship with Nurse Sadler because he likes to see young people enjoying innocent pleasures. His own flirtation with Nurse Sadler and Dr Scott is a reminder that he is a man with very definite physical needs. Ken's humanity is also demonstrated by his sense of humour. He likes to joke around with John and his comments to the nurses are often full of **ironic** wit.

Ken is perhaps a little unfair in his assessment of those he feels oppose him. He fails to acknowledge that the professionalism he so detests may at times be necessary for the proper functioning of an efficient hospital (see **Themes: Professionalism and care**). Neither does he accept that Dr Emerson's motives might spring from benevolent sources.

Given his circumstances, the mental and emotional balance achieved by Ken is extraordinary. The persistence with which he pursues his goals is unwavering. The arguments he uses are convincing both to the other characters in the play and the audience. When he achieves his goal, the sense that he richly deserves his prize is tempered with sorrow that such a complete human being is about to be lost.

## DR EMERSON

Dr Emerson is completely opposed to Ken's plans and will use any available means to prevent his death. Yet in doing what he considers to be the right thing he is prepared to condemn Ken to a lifetime of misery. Emerson acts from principles which apparently seem sound. Yet the rigid application of his beliefs ends up making him an enemy of those around him.

Dr Emerson believes absolutely that it is his duty and his responsibility to keep his patients alive. No one would disagree with this, and most of us would wish to be in the hands of this sort of doctor. His beliefs are such that he is prepared to act aggressively in their defence. He tries to intimidate Ken's solicitor when he first meets him, and he shows no patience with Dr Scott's qualms about administering the Valium. But Dr Emerson's total commitment to duty eventually puts him in the wrong. He is not prepared to be flexible in his approach to Ken's case. He is unwilling to recognise that some patients may not fit into his moral straitjacket. By trying to force Ken to live against his will (a will that is clearly rational),

**Intelligent**
**Unyielding**
**Moralistic**
**Confident**

**DID YOU KNOW?**

In 1994 the British House of Lords stated that 'an adult patient who is competent, and fully informed of the consequences has a right to refuse medical treatment even if such refusal is likely to result in death'.

Dr Emerson is valuing the exercise of his own morality more highly than the independence and well-being of his patient.

Emerson is compared by Ken to Frankenstein (Act I, p. 26), the doctor who meant to create perfection but ended up making a monster. The **metaphor** is a good one. Dr Emerson is a fine example of how the dogged attachment to a set of excellent principles can result in tragedy and bad judgement. Most people would agree with Dr Emerson that a doctor should be 'committed to life' (Act II, p. 46). Very few would be so obstinate in sticking to this belief when confronted with a case like Ken's.

Is it possible to have any sympathy at all with Dr Emerson? He thinks he is doing the right thing, but then so do many whose rigid belief systems cause untold misery. The only real sense in which we can take Emerson's part is if we recognise he may be afraid. He is 'the responsible person here' (Act II, p. 46) and if Ken dies in unusual circumstances it is Emerson who will take the blame. If, after Ken's death, it were established that his actions were indeed the result of insanity, then Dr Emerson's whole livelihood would be at risk. All readers and watchers of the play can sympathise with this. The burden of responsibility often makes people unpopular. But we can only guess that Dr Emerson feels this fear. He never gives any indication of it and our sympathies are therefore tentative.

## DR SCOTT

Dr Scott is the perfect antidote to Dr Emerson. She is warm and sincere, intelligent and, most of all, open-minded. Like Emerson, she starts off with the expectation that Ken will live indefinitely with his injuries and that one of her jobs is to help him adjust. This is where her similarities with Dr Emerson end. The moment Ken begins to express reservations about his life, Dr Scott begins to listen. She responds in the way her training has prepared her – by prescribing a drug – but she is content to adapt this treatment after talking to the person it is going to affect. The more she talks to Ken and later, off stage, Philip Hill, the more convinced she becomes that Ken's decision is the right one. Her role as a doctor, as a carer, becomes that of helping Ken to achieve his goal.

**Thoughtful**

**Flexible**

**Engaged**

**Responsive**

Dr Scott is highly professional in the sense that she is brisk and businesslike and gets on with her work as efficiently as possible. Her professionalism, however, is not of the sort that Ken so despises (see **Themes: Professionalism and care**). Her energetic commitment is the consequence of her desire to achieve results, not to keep patients at a distance. This is clear the moment Ken shows he wants to talk. Dr Scott is prepared to spend time with him and genuinely consider his views. She treats him as he wishes to be treated. She recognises his sanity and the genuine force of his arguments. In the end, she likes him and becomes the only person in the play to address him by his first name (Act II, p. 55).

Dr Scott's humanity ends up by being more important than her job. The white coat, stethoscope and Valium of the opening scenes are replaced at the end with the sympathetic woman who '*turns and moves to* KEN *as if to kiss him*' (Act II, p. 76). She shows that it is more important to respond to patients' needs than to judge them. Clark uses her to illustrate that an active, thoughtful intelligence is more valuable than the rigid application of principles, however noble they may sound. She is, most of all, prepared to accept that patients may better understand their own needs than doctors. This demonstrates humility, a quality that Dr Emerson glaringly lacks.

## SISTER ANDERSON

Sister Anderson is another of those characters who is portrayed by Clark as suffering from the taint of 'professionalism'. Ken doesn't like it because he thinks it is designed to keep patients in their places. To be fair to the hospital staff, however, the kind of attention Ken expects would be impossible to give to everyone. Sister Anderson is always very busy and she simply has too many jobs to do to spend time exchanging dry witticisms with Ken. So her briskness may be excused by a sensitive audience, as, in his fairer moments, it is excused by Ken.

As well as being brisk, Sister Anderson is sharp. She responds quickly and ably to Ken's teasing remarks and remains always his match. She is competent at her job and ensures that those in her command like John and Nurse Sadler do their jobs too. This efficiency causes her to be stereotyped – 'Is she your standard

**EXAMINER'S SECRET**
None of the characters in the play intentionally causes misery even though the consequences of what some of them say and do may be terrible. You will get credit for treating their ideas and actions in a sympathetic way.

**Brisk**
**Efficient**
**Kind**

gorgon?' asks Peter Kershaw (Act II, p. 56) – but in reality she is someone who cares about those she treats. She does not want Ken to end his life and she is upset that he is trying to do so. Yet her opposition to Ken's intentions takes a very different form to Dr Emerson's. Dr Emerson is opposed in principle to Ken's death. Sister Anderson is opposed because she likes Ken and wants him to live. Nevertheless, there is no sense that she ever tries to obstruct Ken or convince him that he should not do as he plans.

Sister Anderson is a likeable character, professional and humane. She reminds us that people we admire and like and respect may sometimes be in complete disagreement with us over the things that matter to us most. In opposing Ken, she demonstrates that those we are ranged against may have more in common with us than we think.

## Dr Travers

**Competent
Knowledgeable
Trusts Dr Emerson**

Dr Travers is Dr Emerson's ally. He does what Emerson says because he trusts his colleague's judgement. In doing so he fails to exercise his own.

Dr Travers explains the provisions of the Mental Health Act to Dr Emerson in order that Ken can be legally detained by the hospital against his own wishes. Dr Travers agrees to appoint a Catholic psychiatrist to assess Ken because such a person will be more likely to oppose suicide. Travers colludes with Emerson in this piece of dubious ethics because he believes that the means justify the ends. In other words, he believes that any method required should be employed to keep Ken alive because Ken's life is all that matters. As we have seen, Ken makes an excellent case against this position, which is repeatedly ignored by Dr Emerson. Travers differs from Emerson because he is a trained psychiatrist and he actually examines Ken. Ken is at his most articulate, sane and convincing during his interview with Dr Travers, yet Dr Travers eventually pronounces him mentally unsound. This is an entirely unwarranted assertion of power by the strong over the weak. Dr Travers, who is not, it appears, a naturally dishonest or cruel person, feels justified in his dishonesty because he believes Ken is wrong to abandon his life.

## MRS BOYLE

Mrs Boyle is the essence of professionalism and Ken detests her for it. She is the embodiment of the 'optimism industry' (Act I, p. 2) that insists on the avoidance of unpleasant facts. She is an expert at overcoming the obstacles and hurdles Ken puts in the way of the purposeful future she envisions for him.

As with Dr Emerson, it is difficult to find fault with Mrs Boyle's initial approach. Most patients in Ken's position presumably want a positive attitude from their carers. They do not want to be told that life is no longer worth living. They want to hear about the options available to them. Mrs Boyle supplies all these things and more. Where she fails, and this is true of Dr Emerson as well, is in her persistence, her refusal to adapt once her patient has demonstrated that he does not fit the expectations. She is relentless; she ignores his reservations; she refuses to accept that his objections are relevant, considered and sane. She will not let him be himself.

Mrs Boyle has the attributes of a very good medical social worker. But she does not adapt when she sees Ken is different, and this is her problem.

**Brisk**
**Professional**
**Patronising**

## NURSE SADLER

Nurse Sadler expresses no real opinion on Ken's case and her role in the play lies elsewhere. She demonstrates, through her relative inexperience, how it is possible to carry out professional duties without necessarily sacrificing compassion and humanity. Ken likes her because she is forthright and he can talk to her on equal terms. Her relationship with John is also attractive to Ken because it stands as a symbol of youthful energies and passions. So simply by being herself – young, healthy, approachable, attractive – Nurse Sadler provides an emblem of everything in life that Ken has been denied. He never resents her for this. But the absence in his own life of what she symbolises is why he wants to die.

**Inexperienced**
**Natural**
**Warm**

## JOHN

Ken says that John is 'Free of guilt ... He's sorry for me but knows ... it isn't his fault' (Act II, p. 62). John is rather different from the other characters in that he is really not concerned with the ethics of

**Sharp-witted**

**Engaging**

**Uncomplicated**

**Tough-minded**

**Persistent**

**Principled**

Ken's case. It is interesting, then, that he makes one of the most pressing yet undeveloped points about it. He says that while children in Africa die of measles for the want of a few pounds, hundreds of pounds a week are spent on giving Ken a life he does not want. 'There's something crazy somewhere' (Act I, p. 16), he concludes.

But John, despite his unusual perceptions, is not really interested in Ken's circumstances. He is interested in his music, Nurse Sadler and the opportunities life affords for humour. He pursues these interests on and off stage throughout the play. His role, therefore, is similar to his eventual girlfriend's. His vitality provides a dramatic contrast with the sterility of Ken's life in the hospital. He reminds an audience of the physicality that Ken has lost. His energy and love of life brings Ken's lack of these things into sharp relief: John is, in his energies, what Ken was. The loss of these energies is so important to Ken that he no longer wishes to live.

## PHILIP HILL

Philip Hill is thoughtful, tough and articulate. He needs to be, because in his first meeting he has to face down Dr Emerson at his most arrogant and dismissive. The fact that he does this with such quiet authority lends much dignity to Ken's case. He responds no differently in his second conversation with Dr Emerson, in the hospital corridor, just before the court hearing. He presents Ken's case with calmness and force. It is not that Ken wishes to undermine a doctor's authority, he says, but that the law must protect people from the arbitrary use of power.

Mr Hill comes to his conclusions in support of Ken after due consideration. Like Dr Scott, he dislikes the outcome of Ken's thoughts but respects his right to arrive at them. Hill therefore respects rationality and is prepared to change his own views if the alternative opinions are persuasive. He refuses to impose his own ethics on others. In these respects he is similar to both Ken and Dr Scott – Ken jokingly calls him 'my surrogate self' (Act II, p. 54) – and utterly different from Dr Emerson.

## JUSTICE MILLHOUSE

Justice Millhouse is indeed just. He listens carefully to all the legal arguments and concludes that the only way to determine Ken's sanity is to listen to the man himself. He is convinced, as Dr Emerson and Dr Travers refuse to be, that Ken is sane and has the right, like all sane people, to shape his own destiny. He supports rationality, logic, sense and sound judgement wherever it may lead. In Ken's case, of course, it will lead to death. This is not a conclusion with which the judge is happy, but he does not obstruct it simply because he dislikes it.

**Consistent**
**Thorough**
**Logical**

## PETER KERSHAW, DR BARR AND ANDREW EDEN

These characters are only important in their presentation of the legal arguments for and against Ken's application. Peter Kershaw is Ken's barrister. During the court hearing he cross-examines Dr Barr. Dr Barr is a psychiatrist from another hospital who has found Ken to be sane. Mr Kershaw and Dr Barr thus present the case that Ken is in control of his mental faculties and should be allowed to end his life. Andrew Eden is the hospital's barrister. During the hearing he cross-examines Dr Emerson, who makes the case for Ken's detention.

 **CHECK THE NET**
You can find out about the difference between solicitors and barristers and the jobs they do at **www.lawsociety. org.uk**. Type 'difference' into the search engine.

## LANGUAGE AND STYLE

Language is skilfully used throughout the play to mark out different characters and situations. The style of speech tells us much about the backgrounds, attitudes and personalities of the people who are using it. Most of the drama is not visual but verbal, the tension and excitement stemming from **dialogue** rather than actions.

### IRONY

**Irony** is characteristic of Ken's speech, particularly early on in the play. 'How are you this morning?' asks Dr Emerson. 'As you see, racing around all over the place', replies Ken (Act I, p. 10). There are many examples of this. Ken uses irony to make his listener take notice. He does not want bland, meaningless small talk with the hospital staff. He wants them to accept that he is paralysed, and he wants them to accept that he does not like it. The use of irony is an excellent way of doing this because it does not imply self-pity. When Ken tells Sister that he has been out skateboarding – and that he was the skateboard (Act I, p. 3) – he is asking Sister to laugh, not to pity. His irony suggests a toughness of attitude and a refusal to descend into trivia. When others come up against it they are forced in some way to acknowledge it. Some people, like Dr Scott, meet it head-on. Ken tells her that his heart is broken in two. 'And I thought it was the first and second heart sounds', rejoins Dr Scott (Act I, p. 7). Ken likes this because it opens the way to conversation that has the potential at least to be interesting and serious. Others, like Dr Emerson, ignore Ken's irony or pretend they do not understand it. They see his observations as dangerous, negative, conducive to depression. They believe that encouraging this sort of thing is bad for Ken. In this, as in other things, they consider themselves better judges of Ken's welfare than the man himself.

Irony is thus a way out for Ken. It makes others listen and it makes them respond. It is spiky and awkward and suggests complicated problems. It is never pathetic.

## PROFESSIONAL LANGUAGE

Those who do not wish to respond to Ken's **ironic** observations can either ignore him or change the subject. This is the essence of a professionalism depicted in this play that refuses to adapt to the particular needs of individual patients. Optimism may well be the right attitude to adopt in most cases, but Ken for one wants more than this.

**CHECK THE BOOK**

In *Amsterdam*, Ian McEwan's Booker Prize winning novel, two friends make a pact to help each other commit suicide if the need arises.

Mrs Boyle is the epitome of professional speech and she uses it repeatedly. Ken is rude to her about Dr Emerson and she replies primly: 'Dr Emerson is a first-rate physician. My goodness, they have improved this room' (Act I, p. 26). She does not want to address the real issue, or at least the issue in which Ken is interested. He wants to talk about the fact that Emerson has created a monster; she will not let him. It is not professional, Mrs Boyle feels, to allow patients to brood on their injuries, so she persists in what she thinks is a motivational way. She infuriates Ken, of course, in just the way that Dr Travers does later on when he adopts the same techniques.

She is keeping Ken at a distance, refusing to listen to what he really wants, imposing upon him her vision of his future. 'All you people have the same technique', says Ken. 'When I say something really awkward you just pretend I haven't said anything at all … your appalling so-called professionalism … is nothing more than a series of verbal tricks to prevent you relating to your patients as human beings' (Act I, p. 29).

Professional language is used when people wish to ignore Ken without appearing to do so. It is a polite insult which Ken never fails to recognise.

## METAPHOR

Ken uses **metaphor** as he uses irony. He wishes to be provocative and colourful. He wants to make people listen and he wants to communicate his dissatisfaction without sounding needy and pathetic. He jokes with John about being on the compost heap (Act I, p. 5) and he tells Dr Emerson that he is a vegetable (Act I, p. 11). He makes repeated references to the more exalted doctors as gods. This fondness for metaphors is typical of the sort of intelligence that enjoys reflecting on the odd comparisons thrown up by experience. It is a further indication of Ken's sharpness and wit. He refuses to be bowed by his injuries, yet neither will he accept their consequences.

## HUMOUR

The bulk of the humour in this play resides either in Ken's dry observations or else in John's more obvious comedy. John's energetic seduction of Nurse Sadler has a slapstick quality and reflects, as always, the vitality and life now denied to Ken. When John first grabs Nurse Sadler by the waist he claims that it was from a patriotic impulse: 'There was this vision in white and blue, then I saw red in front of my eyes. It was like looking into a Union Jack' (Act I, p. 15). When he invites her back to his house he claims it is for an 'anatomy lesson' to help her through her exams (Act I, p. 17). John's language, like his behaviour, is a welcome break from the almost relentless seriousness of the rest of the play.

**DID YOU KNOW?**
The Oregon 'Death with Dignity' law came into effect in 1997. It allows terminally ill patients to gain assistance if they wish to die. So far it is the only American state to have passed such legislation.

## EXCLUSIVITY

Dr Emerson's style of speech is a little different from the other characters. This reflects his detachment from them and his somewhat isolated perspective. The individuality of his language is captured by the way he names people. He calls his male colleagues (like Travers and Barr) by their surnames and he refers to Dr Scott by her first name, Clare, even though she calls him sir. This is indicative of the exclusive sort of education Emerson is likely to have received. It is briskly informal and unsentimental with other males and a little confused about females. It is also authoritarian since it places his female colleagues on a lower, less intimate footing than his male ones. The intimacy with which Emerson talks to his male staff is shown by the one piece of slang he uses in the play. 'Find an old codger like me,' he tells Dr Travers, 'who believes in something better than suicide' (Act II, p. 44). Dr Emerson is the play's authority figure, and his language reflects this.

## PRECISION AND FOCUS

**CHECK THE FILM**

*The Sea Inside (Mar adentro)*, directed by Alejandro Amenábar, portrays a Spanish quadriplegic's battle for the right to end his life with dignity. The film won the Grand Special Jury Prize at the 2004 Venice Film Festival.

As the play develops, the language becomes more precise and focused upon the issues surrounding Ken's case. Ken's discussion with Dr Travers, for example, and Philip Hill's conversation with Dr Emerson before the trial demonstrate a style of language that is extraordinarily focused on the point at hand. Both sides to the argument present their case with absolute conviction and seriousness. The culmination of this trend is obviously the hearing itself, where the language is exclusively to do with the legal arguments one way or the other.

**Now take a break!**

## PART FOUR

## RESOURCES

# HOW TO USE QUOTATIONS

One of the secrets of success in writing essays is to use quotations effectively. There are five basic principles:

**❶** Put inverted commas at the beginning and end of the quotation.

**❷** Write the quotation exactly as it appears in the original.

**❸** Do not use a quotation that repeats what you have just written.

**❹** Use the quotation so that it fits into your sentence.

**❺** Keep the quotation as short as possible.

Quotations should be used to develop the line of thought in your essays. Your comment should not duplicate what is in your quotation. For example:

> **Dr Emerson tells Dr Travers that Ken wants to kill himself:** **'He's determined to kill himself.'** (Act II, p. 44)

Far more effective is to write:

> **Speaking of Ken to Dr Travers, Dr Emerson says: 'He's determined to kill himself.'** (Act II, p. 44)

However, the most sophisticated way of using the writer's words is to embed them into your own sentence:

> **Dr Emerson tells Dr Travers that Ken is 'determined to kill himself'.** (Act II, p. 44)

When you use quotations in this way, you are demonstrating the ability to use text as evidence to support your ideas – not simply including words from the original to prove you have read it.

# COURSEWORK ESSAY

Set aside an hour or so at the start of your work to plan what you have to do.

**EXAMINER'S SECRET**
Keep quotations short and to the point. Lengthy quotations take up time and do not earn extra marks.

- List all the points you feel are needed to cover the task. Collect page references of information and quotations that will support what you have to say. A helpful tool is the highlighter pen: this saves painstaking copying and enables you to target precisely what you want to use.

- Focus on what you consider to be the main points of the essay. Try to sum up your argument in a single sentence, which could be the closing sentence of your essay. Depending on the essay title, it could be a statement about a character: Dr Emerson's morality causes his behaviour to be cruel; an opinion about a setting: The organisation of Ken's room is a tribute to the professionalism he so dislikes; or a judgement on a theme: We must not assume that a wish to die is evidence of insanity.

- Make a short essay plan. Use the first paragraph to introduce the argument you wish to make. In the following paragraphs develop this argument with details, examples and other possible points of view. Sum up your argument in the last paragraph. Check you have answered the question.

- Write the essay, remembering all the time the central point you are making.

- On completion, go back over what you have written to eliminate careless errors and improve expression. Read it aloud to yourself, or, if you are feeling more confident, to a relative or friend.

**EXAMINER'S SECRET**
Communicate ideas clearly and effectively by using a wide vocabulary, including any specialist terms.

If you can, try to type your essay, using a word processor. This will allow you to correct and improve your writing without spoiling its appearance.

## SITTING THE EXAMINATION

Examination papers are carefully designed to give you the opportunity to do your best. Follow these handy hints for exam success:

## BEFORE YOU START

- Make sure you know the subject of the examination so that you are properly prepared and equipped.

- You need to be comfortable and free from distractions. Inform the invigilator if anything is off-putting, e.g. a shaky desk.

- Read the instructions, or rubric, on the front of the examination paper. You should know by now what you have to do but check to reassure yourself.

- Observe the time allocation – and follow it carefully. If they recommend sixty minutes for Question 1 and thirty minutes for Question 2, it is because Question 1 carries twice as many marks.

- Consider the mark allocation. You should write a longer response for 4 marks than for 2 marks.

## WRITING YOUR RESPONSES

Use the questions to structure your response, e.g. question: 'To what extent do you agree with Dr Emerson's attempts to "save" Ken? You should consider: his sense of duty and responsibility; the way he deals with those who disagree with him; and the arguments Ken uses against him.' The first part of your essay will deal with the way Emerson is guided by his beliefs; the second part will consider his very rigid defence of those beliefs; the third part will look at the way Ken's arguments cause us to sympathise more with the patient's view.

- Write a brief draft outline of your response.

- A typical thirty-minute examination essay is probably between 400 and 600 words in length.

- Keep your writing legible and easy to read, using paragraphs to show the structure of your answers.

- Spend a couple of minutes afterwards quickly checking for obvious errors.

**EXAMINER'S SECRET**
Always read the whole examination paper before you start writing.

## WHEN YOU HAVE FINISHED

● Don't be downhearted – if you found the examination difficult, it is probably because you really worked at the questions. Let's face it, they are not meant to be easy!

● Don't pay too much attention to what your friends have to say about the paper. Everyone's experience is different and no two people ever give the same answers.

# IMPROVE YOUR GRADE

## KNOW THE PLAY

**CHECK THE NET**
The artist Tom Phillips has painted several portraits of Brian Clark. You can see them online at **www.tomphillips. co.uk**. Type 'Brian Clark' into the search engine.

It is no use being able to say interesting things about what you've read if you don't know your material inside out. You must get to know as much as you possibly can about the events of the play, its themes and the characters. The best way to do this is first of all to read the play through in class and then on your own. Don't torture yourself with reading the play again and again, though. Going over the same ground repeatedly is boring for most people and not the best way to get the thorough understanding you need. You need to vary your approach.

As a student, the very fact you are reading these words demonstrates that you are prepared to go beyond the text and look for other sources of understanding. That puts you in a minority straight away. If you want to press home your advantage then read more widely still. Check the extra reading and the websites listed in this book. Look for other websites. If you're really involved, chat with other students about the play. The more you read and talk, the more you learn.

**CHECK THE NET**
There is a cast list for the film version of *Whose Life is it Anyway?* on the Internet Movie Database. Go to the home page at **www.imdb.com** and type the title of the play into the search engine.

When you've done your research, go back to the play after a break. Read it again. Have another look at these Notes. You will find that by using different routes into the text you will now understand it far better than you did at first. Think of the play as like a person. You don't know a person by seeing them in one place, in one way and at one time. You get to know them by seeing who they are and how they respond in different situations. It's exactly the same with a work of literature. You don't know it until you've looked at it all ways.

## RESERVE JUDGEMENTS

A big part of knowing a play (again the same is true with a person) is not thinking you know it too soon. Read, read again, research, discuss and wait. Don't pigeonhole the characters before you know them. Don't assume you know immediately what Brian Clark intended when he wrote the play. Playwrights are often surprised and pleased when directors come up with new interpretations of material they themselves were sure they knew inside out. Those least likely to learn are those assured they know enough. Why keep learning if you know all there is to know? The fact, of course, is that you can never know everything about anything important. So don't jump to conclusions. Wait until you've given yourself a good chance to know your material. Your ideas are likely to be far better than they would otherwise have been.

As far as this play is concerned, let Dr Emerson be your inspiration. He was absolutely sure he understood Ken's needs and that he knew precisely what to do. He didn't listen to Ken. He assumed from the first that Ken was mentally unbalanced. He jumped to a conclusion that was later proved to be false. He didn't get to know his subject and he didn't examine it from all angles. Don't make the same mistake yourself.

## DEVELOP YOUR IDEAS

Many students have good ideas about what they have read but then they don't develop them. Imagine you are writing about Dr Scott, for example. It is true to say that she is a kind person, but this is not enough. You need to point out that she uses her intelligence in an active way. She changes her mind as more facts about Ken become available to her. She is prepared to respond to him as a person, despite her professional commitments. She could be accused of misconduct in supporting his desire to die, so her action represents a personal risk. All these things can be contrasted with the way in which Dr Emerson and Dr Travers behave. Use examples to back up your comments about her character. Her ability to adapt her professionalism to the circumstances is shown when she calls Ken by his first name. In her meeting with Emerson she reveals a steely determination that matches her superior colleague's. Use quotations that support your examples.

**EXAMINER'S SECRET**

Brian Clark says: 'in every play I write there's a thousand different plays'. He means that what he writes can be understood in many different ways. If you are prepared to make your own interpretations of the play, then your writing will be original and your grade will be higher.

**EXAMINER'S SECRET**

Familiarise yourself with technical and literary terms and use them in your answers.

In many subjects it is enough simply to find and give the answer. You might have to show how you arrived at your answer, but once you get there you are either right or wrong. This is simply not the case with English and this is why students can sometimes find the subject so frustrating. 'Just tell us what to write' must run through many students' minds as they listen to complicated possibilities to explain this or that element in a play or novel. Literature is speculative and uncertain because life is like that. No one can say for certain what is right or true. What we can do – and those who do it will gain higher grades in exams – is to develop our ideas of what is true. Yes, Dr Scott is kind. That is a true statement but it does not get us very far. If you develop your ideas about Dr Scott, say all you can about her, explore her personality as far as possible, then you will be on your way to writing well about your subject. The more your ideas are developed, the better will be your grade.

## HAVE CONFIDENCE IN YOURSELF

Confidence comes from knowledge and grows naturally the more you discover. The best way to develop confidence is therefore to know the play. This confidence is available to everyone. It is not something automatically reserved for some student elite whose judgements and ideas are perfect. Students with justified confidence are those who have put in the spadework and know their stuff. You too can be like that. Work hard, study your material and the confidence will grow. The more confidence you have, the better your writing will be. Your ideas, if they are supported with reasonable evidence, can stand up against anyone else's. It takes confidence to believe this but it is true.

## ANSWER THE QUESTION

**EXAMINER'S SECRET**

As you are writing keep asking yourself: 'Am I answering the question I've been set?'

The examiner sets a question that is designed to test your knowledge of the play. You bring to bear what you know about a play in writing your answer. If you know the play well, then you are likely to get a good grade. You may get a less impressive grade if you don't answer the question the examiner has set. The examiner may come to the conclusion that you have written interestingly about something that wasn't asked. The suspicion may be that you have done this because you only know one part of the play or because you cannot think on your feet. If you only know one part of the play (and you were hoping for a question that didn't arrive), then this is something you need to sort out before you even start to write. If your mind is not working properly in exam situations, this is something that can be addressed.

To answer examination questions (and coursework questions as well) you do need to be able to think on your feet. In other words, you need to look at what you've been asked, think about it, and then bring your knowledge to bear on answering the exact question. All the information you have about the play needs to be sifted and channelled into that question. Some of what you've spent so long studying will be no use. That is always true and it's part of study. What will be of use needs to be organised to answer your question. Keep the essay question in mind as you write. Ask yourself as you are writing: 'Am I answering the question?' and 'Does what I'm writing now answer what I've been asked?' Make it relevant. If someone asks you directions to your house you don't tell them everything you know about world geography. Be as disciplined in your answers to English questions.

## ORGANISE YOUR ANSWER

Read the question. Think carefully about what it is you are being asked to do. Come to a conclusion about what you've been asked and then start to plan your answer. Include everything that you think is important and nothing that is irrelevant. Imagine your answer as a set of building blocks. Adding another block develops and changes and refines your building. No section should be developed at the expense of another, and each section should fit in appropriately with each other. A building with a complete set of blocks is finished. It's the same with a well-planned, well-organised essay. You need to know how everything will fit with everything else before you start to write.

**EXAMINER'S SECRET**
Divide your essay plan into sections. Make each section into a separate paragraph when you write your response. This technique helps produce an organised answer.

## SAMPLE ESSAY PLAN

Here is an essay plan on *Whose Life is it Anyway?* for you to look at. If you are writing in an exam, you won't be able to make such a

detailed plan, but you do need to follow the basic outlines of what follows. Your own plan will be in note form – you are writing to yourself, after all.

**Do you agree with Judge Millhouse that all the parties involved in Ken's case have 'acted in good faith'?**

Before you even start to write a plan, have a think about what it is you are being asked. In this case, it seems, the question is asking you to talk about how different characters, including Ken, might not have acted properly. If there was no doubt that they had all done the right thing, then the judge would not have felt it necessary to make his statement. With this in mind, you can start to write your plan.

## INTRODUCTION

Say whom you are going to write about. If you are writing about the important decisions surrounding Ken's case, you need only concentrate on the characters making and influencing those decisions. These characters are Ken himself, Dr Emerson, Dr Travers, Dr Scott, Ken's legal team and, at a push, Mrs Boyle. Tell the reader you are going to write about these characters because they are the ones who influence Ken's case. Explain that the characters disagree with one another but that none of them appear to have evil or wicked or misguided motives, despite the fact that death or misery will result if their arguments are successful.

## PART 1

Ken acts in good faith. Can we agree with this? The only way Ken could be said not to be acting in good faith is if he is mentally unbalanced and cannot make decisions rationally. You need to demonstrate through examples and quotations that Ken is completely in control of his own decision-making and thereby acts in a way in tune with his self-interest.

## PART 2

Say that Dr Emerson is opposed to Ken's plans because he considers him mentally unsound. In your first paragraph you have shown that Ken is perfectly sane. So what can explain Dr Emerson's behaviour? His moral code, which says that none of his patients must ever die if he can keep them alive. This is a good moral code, so we might say that Dr Emerson acts in good faith.

## PART 3

But Ken is sane and Dr Emerson is clearly condemning him to a life of imprisonment and misery against his will. Even though he has a 'good' moral code, can we still say he acts in good faith? Dr Emerson is arrogant. He won't listen to others. He pressurises Dr Travers into judging Ken mentally unsound. He considers the implementation of his authority to be more important than the well-being of his patient. I think we may conclude that the judge was hasty in saying that Dr Emerson acted in good faith. He should have been more flexible. His rigidity cannot be seen as good.

## PART 4

Does Dr Scott act in good faith? She is allowing one of her patients to kill himself. Is this right? Yes, because she comes to this conclusion after much soul-searching and from an opposition at the beginning similar to Dr Emerson's. She is convinced of Ken's sanity and she adapts her moral position according to changing discoveries. Dr Emerson might be more moral but she is more humane. In comparison with her humanity, Emerson's morality looks pretty bleak.

**EXAMINER'S SECRET**
Stick to your plan. Students who don't do this often run out of time.

## PART 5

Does Ken's legal team act in good faith? Yes, because – like Dr Scott – they clearly arrive at their position after due consideration of Ken's mental state and the facts of the case. They consider it to be reasonable that a man in control of his mind should be allowed to act upon his conclusions. Give examples of Philip Hill's thinking.

## PART 6

Does Dr Travers act in good faith? Not really. Ken is clearly sane and Dr Travers pretends he is not. The only way Dr Travers can be defended is by saying that he believes the means justify the ends. In other words, Ken should not be allowed to die (the ends) so any means (pretending he is mad) are justified in causing this outcome. Like Dr Emerson, we may say that his good faith is up for discussion.

## PART 7

Mrs Boyle. She acts in good faith because she believes that Ken should be helped to come to terms with his position. Her failing, as with Dr Emerson and Dr Travers, is her inability to adapt when new knowledge (about Ken) becomes available. Then she puts her job, her career, her responsibilities, above Ken's well-being. She doesn't act in bad faith or wickedly but her mental rigidity is harmful.

## CONCLUSION

The judge may be right. All the characters can be said to have acted in good faith. We are hesitant, however, in our judgement of Dr Emerson, Dr Travers and Mrs Boyle. They appear to be using high-minded ethical concern for Ken as a way of ignoring his real needs. They think they know best about his future. Their good faith, we might say, is a good faith we would do better without. Good judgement is a more attractive and more useful quality.

Each different element of the plan should form roughly one paragraph. A plan like this – in note form, don't forget, and much briefer because it is being written to yourself – is the structure of your essay. If you make the plan and then follow it, your writing will be organised, clear and to the point.

**EXAMINER'S SECRET**

Don't panic if the questions aren't the ones you wanted. Use what you know to answer what is there, not what you wish was there. Some of the best answers come from students forced to do this.

## FURTHER QUESTIONS

Write plans to some or all of the following questions. Use the plan above as a guide, but remember that your own plans should be shorter, particularly if you are studying the play as an exam text. You may wish also to write full answers to some of these questions under exam conditions.

**❶** What do you consider are Ken's most important personal strengths?

**❷** Write about the contribution made to the play by three of the following characters: Sister Anderson, Nurse Sadler, John, Philip Hill, Dr Travers.

**3** Why do you think Dr Emerson behaves in the way he does?

**4** Ken tells Mrs Boyle: 'The very exercise of your so-called professionalism makes me want to die'. What does Ken mean by 'professionalism' and why is he so hostile to it? Do you think his attitude is fair?

**5** How do Dr Scott and Dr Emerson differ in their responses to Ken?

**6** Ken has good relationships with Sister Anderson, Nurse Sadler and Dr Scott, the three women he sees regularly. What are the different things he likes about each of them?

**7** What part does humour have in the play?

**8** Ken says: 'to hell with a morality that is based on the proposition that might is right'. What is the importance of morality and power in *Whose Life is it Anyway?*

**9** In what ways is an audience made aware of Ken's 'obvious intelligence'?

**10** Consider the importance of some of the different settings used in the play. Think about Ken's room, Dr Emerson's office, the sluice room, Sister Anderson's office, the road outside the hospital. What impact does each setting have on the action that takes place there?

**DID YOU KNOW?**

*Whose Life is it Anyway?* won the Society of West End Theatres' best play award in 1978.

**Now take a break!**

# LITERARY TERMS

**dialogue** conversation between different characters. This is important in *Whose Life is it Anyway?* since there is very little action

**irony** saying one thing and obviously meaning something different. Ken does this a lot, particularly early on in the play, when he wants to remind people not to take him lightly

**metaphor** when something is described in terms of something else. A comparison made for effect, and not to be read literally. Ken, for example, compares himself to vegetation and compost whilst Dr Emerson is compared with a god. Ken's metaphors demonstrate the lively, irreverent state of his mind

**monologue** a single lengthy speech. Judge Millhouse has an important monologue at the play's conclusion

**parody** a comparison between two events intended to make a mockery of one of them; an exaggerated imitation of something that falls far short of the real thing. Ken makes a joke of his evening feed from Nurse Sadler by pretending to be in a restaurant. John parodies Ken's hearing by pretending to be a judge. In both cases, the parody brings humour to something serious

**stage directions** information given by playwrights for actors and directors in the text of the play. Brian Clark doesn't do it very much but what he does do is sometimes interesting. In the first interchange between Ken and Dr Scott, for example, the actors are instructed that his **irony** should be met with a dry response. This in turn indicates that Clark wants Dr Scott to emerge early on as an intelligent soulmate for her patient

CHECKPOINT 1
- Sister is more brisk and firm in her attitude.
- Nurse Sadler seems friendlier and more willing to become involved in personal discussion.

CHECKPOINT 2
- Ken pretends Sister and Nurse Sadler are massaging and caressing him, when of course there is nothing sexual in what they are doing.
- Sister tells him she is pleased he has 'got on' with Nurse Sadler and Ken tells her he has not quite got this far (p. 3).

CHECKPOINT 3
- Ken likes John because the two of them can talk together as adults on an equal footing.
- Everyone else pities him and he dislikes this.

CHECKPOINT 4
- It suggests he has an extremely intelligent and lively mind.
- It indicates he is not afraid of laughing at his own situation or at those in authority.

CHECKPOINT 5
- The first use is positive. It represents John's hope that one day he will be paid for what he likes doing.
- The second use is entirely negative. It is indicative of an approach to care based on ignoring the real needs of patients whilst pretending to help them.

CHECKPOINT 6
- Dr Emerson considers that his responsibility consists of keeping Ken as fit as possible and alive.
- Catering for his daily care and mental well-being is down to others.
- Most people would agree that Emerson's view of things is reasonable at this point.

CHECKPOINT 7
- Not for many people in Ken's situation, but for Ken it is enough. He sees his impotence as part of a wider physical uselessness.
- Although he accepts that many people in his position could make a life for themselves despite the physical handicaps, he does not want to do so himself.
- Whether others agree with him or not, they are finally forced to accept that it is his decision to make.

CHECKPOINT 8
- It may be that Emerson is more concerned with his new equipment than with subtle arguments about patients' rights.
- Later on he is equally abrupt and dismissive with no justification except his moral certitude.

CHECKPOINT 9
- We see that Dr Scott is a principled person, willing to listen both to the opinions of others and to her own doubts.
- She is also strong enough not to be intimidated by Dr Emerson's authority.

CHECKPOINT 10
- It seems rather creepy. Ken needs to be valued and respected, not parented.
- It is surprising that Dr Scott, an intelligent and sympathetic character, sees Emerson's paternalism as a strength.

CHECKPOINT 11
- Mrs Boyle has lots of work to do and cannot become emotionally involved with her patients. This seems reasonable, but it is infuriating to Ken because personal involvement is exactly what he wants.
- Mrs Boyle would argue that intimacy would stop her doing her job. Ken might reply that intimacy with her patients *was* her job.
- It is possible to have sympathy with both sides of this argument, but it is clear at any rate that Mrs Boyle is rather slow to pick up on Ken's needs.

CHECKPOINT 12
- Ken's **metaphor** portrays Emerson as a clumsy, violent policeman, using his truncheon to enforce his will.
- His tone is playful but the point he makes is serious.
- His weakness puts him at the mercy of the strong.

CHECKPOINT 13
- This question has been debated in the courtrooms of many democracies over the last forty years.
- The legal answer at the moment is that the doctors are obliged to let people like Ken die as long as they are sane.
- Morally speaking, there are some people who would deny Ken his right to die, particularly those religious groups opposed to suicide of any kind in any circumstances.

CHECKPOINT 14
- Ken does not trust his carers to tell him the truth about Philip Hill's decision.
- He is powerless to discover the truth himself.

CHECKPOINT 15
- Dr Emerson believes that wishing not to live is irrational. If the psychiatrists agree with him then he has legal support for his case. If they do not, then he will not allow Ken to die anyway.
- His argument is influenced by conviction not logic. He would defend his position by saying it was his responsibility to do what he knew was right.

CHECKPOINT 16
- It is possible that Dr Emerson is afraid his position will be undermined if Ken dies on his watch. If it could be proved after the event that Ken was not sufficiently rational to make his decision to leave the hospital, then Emerson would be the one to blame. We can therefore sympathise with his position.
- It must be noted, however, that Emerson gives us no real cause to think he is afraid – unless, that is, we take his bullish behaviour as evidence of insecurity.

CHECKPOINT 17
- You might well be very worried. Ken's performance is remarkably rational and sane given his circumstances.
- Travers feels obliged by Emerson to pronounce Ken mentally unsound. In doing this he is no doubt forced to go against his own professional judgement.

CHECKPOINT 18
- Given what we know about Dr Emerson's personality, it seems highly likely that he would take it personally. In other words, he would see it as a failure on his part, a defeat.
- He would never concede that suicide was ultimately the right decision for any of his patients – or indeed that it was a decision any one of his patients could have the authority to make because they would prove their insanity by doing so.

CHECKPOINT 19
- No. By this stage in the play, his relationship with Dr Scott has deepened to one of seriousness and mutual respect.
- His appeal to Nurse Sadler is still playful and flirtatious.

CHECKPOINT 20
- Not really. Ken clearly isn't mad at this point. If he went mad in the longer term then it would be down to the failure of his attempts to leave the hospital.
- Emerson would no doubt take it as evidence that he was right to thwart Ken's will and would not accept that his actions were in any way to blame.

## CHECKPOINT 21

- Ken thinks that Nurse Sadler feels guilty for going out and having a good time while he lies paralysed in a hospital bed.
- This depresses him rather because (as well as everything else he has to endure) he has to cope with being the source of unwanted emotions in others.

## CHECKPOINT 22

- Sister is a likeable character in many ways but she comes across as a bit prim here. She acts as though her feelings about Ken's rejection of her care are the most important aspects of the morning.
- A more generous interpretation of her briskness is to say she is trying to contain her emotions.

## CHECKPOINT 23

- This is a matter of opinion. Suffice to say that many people we consider heroes choose their own death rather than that of their comrades or their children.
- It is typical of Dr Emerson to take a moral stance and then stick to it no matter what.

## CHECKPOINT 24

- It is rational and thoughtful.
- It demonstrates that Ken is completely sane and that Judge Millhouse wants to use reason, not emotion, in coming to his decision.

## CHECKPOINT 25

- This is an interesting moment in the play and one open to interpretation.
- Some directors will have Dr Emerson repenting somewhat, behaving generously in defeat.
- Having lost the battle, he wishes to give his former patient a peaceful death. This places a gently humorous interpretation on Emerson's final words.
- It seems more likely, however, that Emerson is serious. Although Ken has won the legal battle, Emerson feels he has won the moral battle. He still thinks he is in the right.
- Inviting Ken to stay in his room gives Ken, in Dr Emerson's eyes, a chance to recognise his error.
- There is no evidence that Emerson's attitude has changed at all.

## Test yourself (Act i)

1 John

2 Sister

3 Dr Emerson

4 Ken

5 Sister

6 Ken

7 Dr Emerson

8 Nurse Sadler

## Test yourself (Act ii)

1 Ken

2 Dr Emerson

3 Dr Scott

4 Dr Travers

5 Philip Hill

6 Nurse Sadler

7 Sister

8 John

# NOTES

# NOTES

Maya Angelou
*I Know Why the Caged Bird Sings*

Jane Austen
*Pride and Prejudice*

Alan Ayckbourn
*Absent Friends*

Elizabeth Barrett Browning
*Selected Poems*

Robert Bolt
*A Man for All Seasons*

Harold Brighouse
*Hobson's Choice*

Charlotte Brontë
*Jane Eyre*

Emily Brontë
*Wuthering Heights*

Brian Clark
*Whose Life is it Anyway?*

Robert Cormier
*Heroes*

Shelagh Delaney
*A Taste of Honey*

Charles Dickens
*David Copperfield*
*Great Expectations*
*Hard Times*
*Oliver Twist*
*Selected Stories*

Roddy Doyle
*Paddy Clarke Ha Ha Ha*

George Eliot
*Silas Marner*
*The Mill on the Floss*

Anne Frank
*The Diary of a Young Girl*

Robert Cormier
*Heroes*

William Golding
*Lord of the Flies*

Oliver Goldsmith
*She Stoops to Conquer*

Willis Hall
*The Long and the Short and the Tall*

Thomas Hardy
*Far from the Madding Crowd*
*The Mayor of Casterbridge*
*Tess of the d'Urbervilles*
*The Withered Arm and other Wessex Tales*

L. P. Hartley
*The Go-Between*

Seamus Heaney
*Selected Poems*

Susan Hill
*I'm the King of the Castle*

Barry Hines
*A Kestrel for a Knave*

Louise Lawrence
*Children of the Dust*

Harper Lee
*To Kill a Mockingbird*

Laurie Lee
*Cider with Rosie*

Arthur Miller
*The Crucible*
*A View from the Bridge*

Robert O'Brien
*Z for Zachariah*

Frank O'Connor
*My Oedipus Complex and Other Stories*

George Orwell
*Animal Farm*

J. B. Priestley
*An Inspector Calls*
*When We Are Married*

Willy Russell
*Educating Rita*
*Our Day Out*

J. D. Salinger
*The Catcher in the Rye*

William Shakespeare
*Henry IV Part I*
*Henry V*
*Julius Caesar*
*Macbeth*
*The Merchant of Venice*
*A Midsummer Night's Dream*
*Much Ado About Nothing*
*Romeo and Juliet*
*The Tempest*
*Twelfth Night*

George Bernard Shaw
*Pygmalion*

Mary Shelley
*Frankenstein*

R. C. Sherriff
*Journey's End*

Rukshana Smith
*Salt on the snow*

John Steinbeck
*Of Mice and Men*

Robert Louis Stevenson
*Dr Jekyll and Mr Hyde*

Jonathan Swift
*Gulliver's Travels*

Robert Swindells
*Daz 4 Zoe*

Mildred D. Taylor
*Roll of Thunder, Hear My Cry*

Mark Twain
*Huckleberry Finn*

James Watson
*Talking in Whispers*

Edith Wharton
*Ethan Frome*

William Wordsworth
*Selected Poems*

*A Choice of Poets*

*Mystery Stories of the Nineteenth Century including The Signalman*

*Nineteenth Century Short Stories*

*Poetry of the First World War*

*Six Women Poets*

For the AQA Anthology:
*Duffy and Armitage & Pre-1914 Poetry*

*Heaney and Clarke & Pre-1914 Poetry*

*Poems from Different Cultures*

Margaret Atwood
*Cat's Eye*
*The Handmaid's Tale*
Jane Austen
*Emma*
*Mansfield Park*
*Persuasion*
*Pride and Prejudice*
*Sense and Sensibility*
William Blake
*Songs of Innocence and of Experience*
Charlotte Brontë
*Jane Eyre*
*Villette*
Emily Brontë
*Wuthering Heights*
Angela Carter
*Nights at the Circus*
*Wise Children*
Geoffrey Chaucer
*The Franklin's Prologue and Tale*
*The Merchant's Prologue and Tale*
*The Miller's Prologue and Tale*
*The Prologue to the Canterbury Tales*
*The Wife of Bath's Prologue and Tale*
Samuel Coleridge
*Selected Poems*
Joseph Conrad
*Heart of Darkness*
Daniel Defoe
*Moll Flanders*
Charles Dickens
*Bleak House*
*Great Expectations*
*Hard Times*
Emily Dickinson
*Selected Poems*
John Donne
*Selected Poems*
Carol Ann Duffy
*Selected Poems*
George Eliot
*Middlemarch*
*The Mill on the Floss*
T. S. Eliot
*Selected Poems*
*The Waste Land*
F. Scott Fitzgerald
*The Great Gatsby*

E. M. Forster
*A Passage to India*
Charles Frazier
*Cold Mountain*
Brian Friel
*Making History*
*Translations*
William Golding
*The Spire*
Thomas Hardy
*Jude the Obscure*
*The Mayor of Casterbridge*
*The Return of the Native*
*Selected Poems*
*Tess of the d'Urbervilles*
Seamus Heaney
*Selected Poems from 'Opened Ground'*
Nathaniel Hawthorne
*The Scarlet Letter*
Homer
*The Iliad*
*The Odyssey*
Aldous Huxley
*Brave New World*
Kazuo Ishiguro
*The Remains of the Day*
Ben Jonson
*The Alchemist*
James Joyce
*Dubliners*
John Keats
*Selected Poems*
Philip Larkin
*The Whitsun Weddings and Selected Poems*
Christopher Marlowe
*Doctor Faustus*
*Edward II*
Ian McEwan
*Atonement*
Arthur Miller
*Death of a Salesman*
John Milton
*Paradise Lost Books I & II*
Toni Morrison
*Beloved*
George Orwell
*Nineteen Eighty-Four*
Sylvia Plath
*Selected Poems*
Alexander Pope
*Rape of the Lock & Selected Poems*

William Shakespeare
*Antony and Cleopatra*
*As You Like It*
*Hamlet*
*Henry IV Part I*
*King Lear*
*Macbeth*
*Measure for Measure*
*The Merchant of Venice*
*A Midsummer Night's Dream*
*Much Ado About Nothing*
*Othello*
*Richard II*
*Richard III*
*Romeo and Juliet*
*The Taming of the Shrew*
*The Tempest*
*Twelfth Night*
*The Winter's Tale*
George Bernard Shaw
*Saint Joan*
Mary Shelley
*Frankenstein*
Bram Stoker
*Dracula*
Jonathan Swift
*Gulliver's Travels and A Modest Proposal*
Alfred Tennyson
*Selected Poems*
Alice Walker
*The Color Purple*
Oscar Wilde
*The Importance of Being Earnest*
Tennessee Williams
*A Streetcar Named Desire*
*The Glass Menagerie*
Jeanette Winterson
*Oranges Are Not the Only Fruit*
John Webster
*The Duchess of Malfi*
Virginia Woolf
*To the Lighthouse*
William Wordsworth
*The Prelude and Selected Poems*
W. B. Yeats
*Selected Poems*
*Metaphysical Poets*